HOPE
UNDERGROUND

The 34 Chilean Miners – A Story of Faith and Miracles

By Carlos Parra Díaz

as told to Mario Veloso and Jeanette Windle

Roseville, CA

Contact:
Amazing Facts
PO Box 1058
Roseville, CA 95678
800-538-7275
www.AFbookstore.com

Scripture quotations, unless otherwise specified, are taken from The Holy Bible, New International Version®, NIV® Copyright © 1973, 1978, 1984, 2011 by Biblica, Inc.™ Used by permission. All rights reserved worldwide.

ISBN 978-0-9869799-5-8

Cover design: Ian Jamieson

Interior design and typeset: Katherine Lloyd, The DESK

This book is dedicated to Jesus Christ,
the greatest Rescuer of all time

ACKNOWLEDGMENTS

Above all, I thank God for performing this great miracle and for giving me the privilege of being a witness to it.

Thank you to all the Christians who joined our prayer chain, earnestly praying for the miners' rescue.

My deepest gratitude goes to my wife Gloria, my children, Malaguías and Belén, for supporting me throughout the time I spent at Camp Hope.

I thank my father, Luis, and my mother, Ester, for sowing in me the seed of the love of God.

Thank you to the leaders of my church in the North Chile Mission for allowing me to dedicate my time to serving at Camp Hope as well as for providing the 33 miniature Bibles sent to the miners.

And finally, my thanks goes to Marcos Cruz who worked hard to create this book.

CONTENTS

PROLOGUE

Planet Earth holds few places less conducive to human habitation than the Atacama Desert. Encompassing more than 100,000 square kilometers, this region covering the northern third of Chile has the reputation of being the driest place on earth. Much of its vastness has never recorded rain.

This is no Sahara Desert, with gently rolling golden sand dunes easy on the eye, but a jumble of barren, windswept plateaus, brown ridges of rock, salt flats, and lava flows, all as wrinkled and broken as a lunar landscape. Temperatures can reach upwards of 35 degrees Celsius (95° Fahrenheit) under a relentless, unshielded sun, then plunge to freezing with nightfall. Unwary travelers venturing into its waterless wastes can quickly fall victim to disorientation and dehydration, wandering around until their own sun-bleached bones have been added to the desert's landscape.

But the desert holds beauty too. The glistening white of snow-capped Andes peaks edging its eastern border. A rhythmic curl of Pacific surf defining its long western coastline. Odd-shaped rock formations rearing stark geometric silhouettes against a fiery sunset. The jeweled brilliance of star constellations against a vast night sky undimmed by atmospheric moisture or man-made illumination. Fragile desert flowers opening pink, yellow, purple, and white petals to dawn's brief seaborne dew.

And there is treasure too. Lots of it. Which is why for all its desolation, the Atacama Desert has become home to more than a million human habitants. Under the bleak surface, buried deep in its rock veins, lie some of the planet's largest deposits of copper, silver, gold, and sulfur nitrate. Dotting the desert are the mines, either still working or abandoned, where for more than two centuries human beings have toiled to bring that treasure to the surface.

Today mining remains Chile's chief export industry. Mines operated by Codelco, the state-owned mining company, include some of the largest and best-equipped on the planet. But San José Mine was not one of these. A modest, independently-owned operation about fifty kilometers from Copiapó, a regional capital, the San José Mine had produced a steady flow of copper and gold ore since its first shaft was excavated in 1889. Its owning entity, San Esteban Mining Company, was also a modest entity, San José its only working mine. If San José's network of tunnels, shafts, surface buildings, and heavy equipment drew occasional media attention, it was for a lengthy history of safety violations, accidents, and cave-ins—enough that in 2007, the government mining safety board had ordered its closure.

But by mid-2010, San José Mine had already been reopened for more than a year. Inside the cavernous mouth of the mine, a narrow roadway corkscrewed downward for more than six kilometers, permitting work vehicles and heavy equipment to reach the lowest levels of the mine. Decades of ore extraction had penetrated the mountainside to a depth of over 700 meters (2300 feet), creating a labyrinth of tunnels, chambers, and shafts so extensive that some mine safety officials described it later as "Swiss cheese." At that depth, temperatures topped 33 degrees C (90° F). Underground water seepage dripped down walls and pooled in chambers, raising moisture levels to almost 100 percent relative humidity.

Still, Chilean miners were a tough breed, accustomed to difficult working conditions. On August 5, 2010, one shift of miners had clocked in at the lower level, carrying out their daily tasks of blasting, removing the ore with pickaxes, and scooping it up for ferrying to the surface. A second group was working near the mine entrance. The miners' normal 2 p.m. lunch break was still twenty minutes away. But on the lower level, a stalled truck had halted operations. As mechanical technicians arrived from the surface to tinker on the engine, the miners headed to a nearby emergency shelter for an early lunch. This was literally just a reinforced chamber dug into the mountain which offered some benches for sitting.

They were still filtering in when a sharp crack of sound sent shock waves through their gathering place. Abruptly, the rigged electrical illumination went dark. Though the miners could not know, almost exactly halfway between where they waited and the surface, a massive chunk of the granite mountainside, measuring more than a hundred meters across and weighing over 700,000 tons, had just "sat," which in mining terminology meant that it had lost the battle with gravity that kept it suspended above hollowed-out tunnels and chambers and had settled downward, smashing through walls and ceilings below, including those of the main ramp.

Aftershocks unleashed dozens of avalanches, collapsing passageways and shafts. Battling a boiling storm of dust and debris, the group of miners working near the entrance made it safely outside. But the lower level party was now trapped on the far side of that colossal rock collapse. Two men from this shift were not near the emergency shelter but were driving a cargo truck from a workshop on a higher level down to join the others. They heard a loud crash as a huge slab of rock collapsed from the ceiling behind them, blocking off the four-meter-wide tunnel. Worried that this was only the beginning of more avalanches, the driver sped up, heading toward the safety of the emergency shelter.

Suddenly in the twin yellow beams of the headlights, both men caught sight of an astonishing spectacle. A small white butterfly was fluttering across the tunnel. What could the tiny insect possibly be doing at this depth of more than half a kilometer beneath the surface?

The driver instinctively hit the brakes. At that very instant, they were suddenly enveloped in an avalanche of dirt and pebbles so dense not even their vehicle's headlights could pierce the haze. The butterfly was gone. Had they dreamed it? But there was no further time to consider the matter. Like so many dominoes falling one after another, aftershocks were now shaking loose huge slabs of tunnel walls and roof all around them.

By evening, not only the mining authorities but the media had been made aware of the disaster at San José Mine. According to the work roster, thirty-four men ranging in age from 19 to 63 were now entombed almost a kilometer underground. Of these, five were contracted mechanics and mining technicians, visiting that day to carry out needed repairs; they normally would not even be down in the mine.

Or were there actually only thirty-three? Some rumors said that not all the miners had showed up to work that day. In either case, were any of the men still alive, or had the lower mine levels collapsed as well? If any were alive, how long could they possibly survive in those black depths with limited air and food?

Within twenty-four hours, family members of the miners had mounted a vigil outside the mine entrance, their staked-out tents and tarps becoming known in following weeks as *Campamento Esperanza* or Camp Hope. Joining them were rescue workers, medical personnel, politicians, and experts, along with humanitarian and religious organizations.

And media crews—lots of them—as the world's attention zeroed in on the catastrophe.

So began the saga of what has since been hailed as the greatest mine rescue of all time. For the next sixty-nine days, not only the families but more than a billion people around the world watched the unfolding of this tense human drama in the middle of the Atacama Desert. They not only watched but prayed. And their prayers were heard. In the end only thirty-three miners emerged from the depths of San José Mine. But their testimony left no doubt of a thirty-fourth Presence in their midst during the entirety of their ordeal. As one miner expressed later when contact was reestablished: "There are actually thirty-four of us, because God has never left us down here."

I myself was not one of the thirty-three miners trapped by

the cave-in. Nor was I a family member of any of them. I had no prior connection to the owners of the mine or the Chilean government. In fact, there was nothing in my past life story to place me in the midst of such a drama—nothing beyond a personal relationship with the God who had created this very mountain in which thirty-three men had been entombed, a God who is in complete control of every situation. And for reasons known only to Him, certainly a mystery to me at that time, God chose in His providence to place me in close proximity to the tragedy almost from its first hours.

But if there is one thing that has been clear to me since the day God called me to serve Him, it is that our heavenly Father does nothing without purpose. He had a purpose in all that would eventually transpire in the depths of San José Mine as well as on its surface. And as events unfolded, bit by bit I began to understand just why God had brought me to this place at this time.

When I first arrived at the San José Mine shortly after the collapse, I was part of a volunteer group of local Christian clergy from the nearby town of Copiapó. Since I was a pastor of Copiapó's Seventh-day Adventist congregation, the disaster had occurred within the boundaries of what that great Christian leader John Wesley termed "my parish." So whether or not the trapped miners were "sheep" of my particular church "flock," I could not remain indifferent to their tragedy. All that mattered was that as fellow human beings, these men were my neighbors, my brothers. In light of this, I felt responsible to do whatever I could to help.

When I arrived, together with my fellow pastors, I was one among many coworkers committed to offering any resources at our disposal to help the families of the trapped miners. I never sought a position of spiritual leadership; my desire was only to serve. But as other volunteers came and went, God called me to lay aside all other responsibilities, dedicating myself to the physical, emotional, and spiritual needs of a new congregation, the residents of Camp Hope. And so within the first few days, I found myself christened with the unofficial title of "chaplain of Camp Hope."

While my thoughts and prayers were constantly with the men buried 700 meters below us—dead or alive, we did not yet know—my responsibility as chaplain was most of all to their loved ones waiting on the surface. I wanted to make a difference in their lives, to relieve their suffering in any way I could. But by the time I left more than two months later, it was my own life that had been changed forever.

In fact, all of us who played a role, however small, in this incredible human drama—not just the miners and their families, but rescue crews, mining personnel, political figures, media, and countless volunteers—would later testify how this experience so deeply impacted our lives that we simply cannot stop talking about it. We have to share what happened to us with others. We speak about it at gatherings of friends, in public forums, through media interviews. Some have already written down their own story in book form.

We tell the same stories again and again. Stories of terrible hardship and great courage underground. Of stunning engineering achievements and scientific ingenuity on the surface. Family dramas, both distressing and heartwarming. Moments of near despair and ultimate triumph.

But there is another side to this story that needs to be told, a spiritual side. No account of the greatest mine rescue of all time would be complete without telling the stories of faith discovered and hope shared. Stories of unexpected miracles; of differences laid aside, whether in church or denomination, to join together as brothers and sisters of one common faith unified in one common cause. Stories of fervent prayers directed heavenward in count-less languages by tens of millions around the world, all offering a single, united plea to God: that this rescue operation would have a happy ending.

There can be no denying that prayer and faith and divine intervention played as significant a role in the survival and rescue of the thirty-three San José miners as the extraordinary scientific expertise of the engineers, the unrelenting determination of the rescue crews, and the capable leadership shown by the Chilean government.

This is the story in which I was privileged to participate dur-ing my time as "chaplain of Camp Hope." And I will never be the same for it. So I too am impelled to share my experience with others. As you take this book now in hand to read my story, may its pages offer unequivocal testimony that in this twenty-first cen-tury, faith still does move mountains.

1

THE JOURNEY BEGINS

My own journey of faith did not begin August 5, 2010, on the dusty slopes of San José Mine, but almost forty-three years earlier and far to the south. I was born Carlos Roberto Parra Díaz on September 15, 1967, in the small, rural community of Coelemu, located 500 kilometers south of Chile's capital city, Santiago. In complete contrast to the Atacama Desert where I would one day find myself, Coelemu is a richly fertile region of rolling hills, eucalyptus forests, green pastures and cultivated fields, fruit orchards, and grape vineyards. Nearby winds the placid waterway of the Itata River.

The family into which I was born was of modest means. My father, Luis Parra, worked at many types of manual labor within the lumber industry, the region's primary export. My mother, Ester, stayed busy running our household and rearing nine children, of whom I was one of the youngest. We lived in a small house built of wood that faced onto an unpaved dirt lane. If cramped for such a large family, we could always retreat outside to a sizable patio filled with fruit trees and a grape arbor. There my siblings and I played, climbing trees, running among the grapevines, driving tiny model cars in the dirt.

My parents were devout Christians, and from my earliest childhood I attended a local evangelical church where I grew up hearing Bible stories and singing hymns and choruses. Our small town was privileged to have both a primary and a secondary school, where my siblings and I attended. The flow of life in Coelemu was unhurried and serene.

Yet I was not always happy. As one of the youngest in a large family, I constantly battled low self-esteem. I had been taught the good news of salvation through Jesus Christ. I believed in the existence and power of a Creator God. But I had never placed my own faith in Jesus Christ or made any personal commitment to follow my Creator.

When I graduated from secondary school at age seventeen, there were no funds available for further education. In fact, no one in my family had ever gone on to university. I had done well in school and dreamed of a higher education. But without the necessary funds, I headed instead to the nearest city to look for work.

Seventy kilometers south of Coelemu, Concepción is Chile's second largest metropolitan center with a population of almost a million people. One of my older brothers, Claudio, had already moved there. Boarding in his home, I quickly found a job. I worked hard, sending part of my earnings home to help my parents, saving what I could in hopes I might be able to study again someday. I made friends.

But I soon also turned my back on the Christian upbringing my parents had provided for me. The big city was filled with temptations for a young man out on his own for the first time. When I was not working, my days soon became a round of parties, dances, and other entertainments of which my parents would certainly not have approved. Church attendance was something of the past.

Once a month or so, I would travel home. My parents had no idea how my life had changed. They were simply happy their son had found work and was building a future for himself. In contrast, despite all the excitement of city life, I was not happy at all. By age nineteen, I had fallen into a deep depression. While I could point to nothing specifically wrong, my life seemed to be spiraling out of my control. I began to question whether God even existed. My self-esteem had hit rock bottom. I had a job, friends, and all my needs supplied. But there seemed no purpose to my existence, no reason to keep living.

By a certain evening when I was nineteen years old, I had come to a drastic decision: I would take my own life. I'd gone out that evening to party with one of my friends. But I could not make myself enjoy the festivities. Offering an excuse to leave my friend, I headed toward the railroad tracks cutting through that part of the city, thinking to throw myself in front of a passing train.

That particular night was clear of clouds, the stars bright against a black sky. It had been a long time since I'd thought of the God in whom my parents had raised me to believe, the

Almighty Creator of the Universe. But as I lifted my eyes to that star-strewn sky, it was as though I glimpsed in the soft glitter of the constellations far above me a peace that I had not been able to find anywhere below on earth—a peace so vast and breathtaking, it brought sharply to my mind the presence of the God I'd learned of as a child, His pardon, His peace.

In desperation, I cried out in the direction of those stars, "God, if You are really there, please forgive my sins, and give me another chance to live."

The answer that came was not thunder from heaven, but I heard its words as audibly as though spoken aloud. "Carlos, I will give you another opportunity to live. But you must live that life for Me."

I dropped my gaze from the glittering expanse of the night sky. But the moment I started looking at the darkness all around, despair once again overwhelmed me. I now know that this was a direct attack from Satan. *You are worthless*, he was murmuring in my mind. *You would be better off taking your own life.*

But the God who had created those constellations and spoken to me from heaven did not abandon me now. Before I could make any rash move, the friend I'd walked out on came rushing up. Somehow he'd sensed my earlier desperation. Worried, he'd been looking for me in all the places we usually hung out. He insisted on escorting me home to my brother's house.

By now it was late at night. My brother Claudio let me in and told me to go to bed. We'd talk in the morning. Still battling despair, I went to my room. There I spotted a New Testament lying on a shelf. I couldn't sleep, so I picked up the New Testament and began leafing through its pages. I don't even remember what passages I read. But in those pages, I caught a glimpse of the same supernatural peace that I'd sensed in the stars. It was as though God was speaking to me again, giving me a direct confirmation that the earlier conversation we'd had was real and that He had forgiven all the wrong things I'd done over those last two years.

Going to bed at last, I slept like a small child, without stirring. When I awoke the next morning, I knew I was a new person, born again. From that day, I committed myself to follow God with all my heart.

"Almighty God, as I asked, You have given me a new chance to live," I prayed. "Now I surrender my life to do Your will. Guide me wherever it is that You want me to serve. Let me live to exalt Your name among all nations."

My next step was to find a local church where I could once again hear and study God's Word. Locating one some distance away within the city of Concepción, I attended there for the next year or so. Then new neighbors moved next door to my brother Claudio's house where I was still living. They were Seventh-day Adventist missionaries, a denomination I had never heard of at that time. They were friendly and kind. Within a short time, they'd volunteered to teach a Bible study in our neighborhood, which I began attending with my sister-in-law, Claudio's wife. After three months of intensive Bible study, both of us made the decision to be baptized as a witness of our faith. On June 24, 1989, I surrendered my life in baptism. I was twenty-one years old.

From the moment I'd placed my faith in God, I'd committed my life to serve Him. But I had no thoughts at that time of ever becoming a pastor or missionary. By then I'd found a good job as an administrative aide in a bank. But I still dreamed of one day getting a higher education. Then our neighbors told me about the Adventist University in nearby Chillán, a city about a hundred kilometers east of Coelemu.

"But I have no funds for university study," I immediately responded.

That didn't matter, the missionaries informed me. Then they explained to me the Adventist University's unique system of self-financing. Students could work one year for the university and then attend free the next year, alternating work and study years until they'd achieved their chosen degree. With great excitement, I enrolled, planning to study accounting, a career that would allow me not only to provide for myself, but to help my family. But by the end of my first year working for the university, God had made it clear that He was calling me into full-time ministry. When I finally started my university studies in 1991, it was in the field of theology rather than accounting.

For the next seven years, I alternated between working and studying. My employment for the university was as a colporteur, distributing and selling Christian literature door to door all over the city as well as in surrounding towns and villages. God had now made clear His calling on my life. But I did not want to follow that calling alone. I began to pray that God would bring into my life the marriage partner He had for me. For five years I prayed, not only that God would prepare the right wife for me, but that He would prepare me as a godly husband for that wife.

Then in my third year of studies, I found myself in Santiago, the capital city of Chile. Part of the course requirements for third-year theology students was to conduct an evangelistic campaign. Among the volunteers helping at the church where I'd been assigned to preach was an attractive young woman named Gloria Angélica Montoya. From a third-generation Christian home, Gloria was a committed Christian herself, deeply involved in children's and youth ministry within her church. She also worked full-time as a nursing assistant at a local psychiatric clinic.

The following year was one of those in which I was not studying. I stayed on in Santiago, working in the literature ministry and also getting to know Gloria better. It was not long before we both recognized how much we'd come to love each other. Both of us had complete peace that God was calling us together as life partners.

Gloria and I were married in the summer of 1996. We returned from Santiago to Chillán for my last year of theological studies. I graduated in 1998 and spent the next year doing a ministry apprenticeship in Concepción. Then Gloria and I returned to Santiago, where for the next five years I served as pastor and missionary overseeing a group of churches in the Santiago metropolitan area. By this time God had given Gloria and me two beautiful children: my son Carlos Malaquías (Malachi), who at the time of this book's writing is thirteen years old, and my daughter Belén, who is now ten.

In 2003, we moved again as a family to Chile's beautiful Viña del Mar region, famous for its vineyards and beaches. Once again, I served as pastor and missionary to a group of churches scattered around the area. Traveling from one to another, I would preach God's Word, teach and counsel church members, and spearhead evangelistic outreach into each community.

It was 2009 when I was asked if I would move from the Viña del Mar region to serve as an area coordinator in the northern city of Copiapó. Moving from the lush vegetation that I'd known all my life in southern Chile to the barren wastelands of the Atacama Desert would be a shock, I knew. But I also knew God was calling me to accept this new ministry challenge. In Copiapó I would have under my supervision nine churches, including a Gypsy *kangiri*, as this Romany people group called their church assemblies, in the small community of Paipote eight kilometers from Copiapó.

The regional capital of Copiapó is a community of about 130,000 inhabitants just beyond where Chile's southern "green zone" gives way to the Atacama Desert. Its main industrial base is the copper, silver, and gold ore dug out of numerous mines in the surrounding area. A large copper smelter in nearby Paipote employs many local residents. Unexpectedly in such an arid zone, the second main source of employment is agricultural production. From my first visit to Copiapó, I was pleasantly surprised to find the town a green oasis, with irrigation for citrus and olive trees, vineyards, and vegetable crops coming from subterranean water sources deep beneath the thirsty surface.

Beyond the irrigated zones, the barrenness of a region that does not receive a single drop of rain is immediately evident. Since my childhood in Coelemu, surrounded by forest-cloaked hills, climbing has been one of my favorite pastimes. Once I'd begun my ministry, I'd made a practice in each new place to which God moved us of finding a nearby hill to climb where I can be alone with God and pray. I was encouraged in doing so by the recognition that I was following Jesus' own example of retreating in solitude to the mountains to spend time with His heavenly Father.

Shortly after arriving in Copiapó, I climbed to the top of a high hill overlooking the city, a peak dubbed by local residents *Cerro de la Cruz*, or Mountaintop of the Cross. The reason for its name was clear as I climbed. At the very summit of the hill, a large white cross rose against the cloudless blue backdrop of the sky.

As I reached the foot of the cross, a Bible verse rose to my thoughts that God had placed in my heart and mind since the very beginning of my ministry. The words were Jesus' own as He foretold how He would soon die upon a cross: "And I, when I am lifted up from the earth, will draw all people to myself" (John 12:32).

Ever since God had called me to serve Him in full-time ministry, my greatest desire had been to see the eyes of everyone drawn to Jesus Christ, to see my Savior exalted among all nations. As I stood there praying over the city of Copiapó and the new ministry to which God had called me, I added a very specific and bold prayer request. I prayed that God would open the door for me to preach His good news of redemption through Jesus Christ, not just in the city of Copiapó, but across the entire region of Atacama, throughout all Chile, and—if in God's sovereign will I was given opportunity—one day even to the rest of the world beyond Chile's borders.

Over the next months I was very busy in my new ministry responsibilities, visiting each of the nine churches assigned to my administration, working and praying with both adults and youth for revival in the church. Together as a united body of believers, we prayed that God would show us how we could make a difference in this city and region for Christ.

Meanwhile, my family had settled in well, my children quickly making new friends at a local Adventist school they attended. When we had free time, we enjoyed hiking the hills around Copiapó as a family. But whenever I could find time, I would climb alone to the white cross on the top of Cerro de la Cruz. Each time I would pray again the prayer I'd offered up on that first day.

Never did I dream that within eighteen months of the first time I climbed that hillside, God would provide a wonderful answer to that bold prayer I'd made, opening the doors for me to speak His gospel, not just throughout the Atacama region and all of Chile, but across the entire world.

2

TRAGEDY STRIKES

W hen I received a call on Friday, August 6, 2010, I was at first taken by surprise. Most of the residents of Copiapó were already aware of the tragedy that had occurred the day before at the nearby San José Mine. But I'd been so busy in recent days with my duties as pastor and missionary that I hadn't even bothered to pay any attention to the news. Then I received the call from Pastor Francisco Briseño, president of our church association for the northern region of Chile.

Without any preamble, he demanded, "Do we have any church members among the miners trapped by the cave-in over at San José Mine?"

"What cave-in?" I answered.

"What do you mean, what cave-in?" he exclaimed in clear astonishment. "Didn't you watch the news last night? There's been a massive rock collapse over at San José Mine, and now thirty-four miners are trapped a full 700 meters below the surface. No one knows yet if they were all buried by the collapsed rock or if they are alive but trapped on the far side of the rock fall."

Surprised and concerned, I immediately agreed to see what I could find out. Calling up the leaders of each area church under my responsibility, I quickly discovered that no one from their congregations was among the missing miners. All of my own spiritual flock were safe. But this only meant that there were men trapped down there in the mine from some other denomination, or perhaps even from no church at all, who now found themselves in grave danger or were already dead. So my concern did not diminish.

What can I do here to help? I asked myself.

For the moment all I could do was to follow the news story that was now being broadcast nonstop on all the different media outlets. According to the reports, an entire crew consisting of thirty-four miners had been working the previous afternoon in the lowest level of the mine when around 2 p.m. a massive rock collapse had left them trapped below without any means of communication to the outside world. No one had any idea what had happened to them. Everything possible to rescue them was being done.

This same basic news account was repeated over and over with minimal variation. TV channels, radio stations, and newspapers were all offering the same information about the events at the San José Mine. All I knew of this particular mine was that it was a relatively small operation producing copper, gold, and silver in the Atacama Desert around fifty kilometers north of Copiapó. But I could guess that if any of the miners were still alive, they would be suffering greatly from the intense heat, darkness, and isolation in which they'd find themselves at that deep level where they were last said to have been working.

The next day, Saturday, August 7, was the third day since the tragedy. By this point, multiple rescue teams had been working around the clock, trying to reach the trapped miners by alternative routes that would allow them to bypass the main rock collapse. But at each attempt, they'd found the path blocked with rubble or the passageway too dangerously unstable to risk sending more men forward. The best remaining option was a ventilation shaft that stretched all the way down to the level where the miners had last been working. Rescue crews had descended into the ventilation shaft to see if they could reach the trapped miners through one of the other tunnels with which the shaft intersected.

The hope to which family members clung was that San José Mine had an emergency shelter prepared for just such an event as this down at one of the lower levels of the mine near where the crew had been working. A room of about fifty square meters dug into solid rock, the shelter held emergency supplies of food, water, and basic medicines along with at least one oxygen tank. If the trapped miners had made it to the shelter, they just might be all sitting there safely, waiting for rescue to arrive. The bad news was that the supplies kept there were designed to maintain a group of no more than ten men for three days at most.

By now their story had galvanized the entire nation of Chile. Both the miners' own families and the Chilean public following the story on the news were demanding that the mine owners and government authorities undertake whatever effort and expense would be necessary to rescue these men. The Chilean president,

Sebastian Piñera, and his recently appointed minister of mines, Laurence Golborne, had both been in Ecuador at a summit with other regional heads of state when they received news of the tragedy. Both cancelled their appointments and flew back to Chile. A Chilean Air Force helicopter had flown Minister Golborne out to San José Mine to assess the situation.

For myself, God had begun to make clear just what He had for me to do in this situation. That day I received another phone call dealing with the trapped miners. This time it was from one of the leaders of the Association of Evangelical Pastors of Copiapó, an organization of which I was a member as a district supervisor of the area's Adventist churches.

My colleague explained the reason for his call. "Pastor Parra, we'd like to go as a group to the mine to pray for the families and to ask that God grant the miracle of keeping these trapped miners alive."

So we went, a total of fifteen pastors. A narrow, winding road led up to the mine site, set among a labyrinth of low, barren hills thrusting up from the flat desert. The mine itself was a narrow, cavernous opening dug into a hillside. This was surrounded by mounds of crushed gray rock, debris from the mining operation.

The scene we encountered at first seemed chaotic, yet despite the bustle of activity, there was a surprising level of order to the undertakings. Normally, the mine was not a crowded place, its entire work force only about 300 employees with less than a hundred men working the mine at any given time. But now the entire site was a jostling swarm of people. Family members had set up camp not far from the entrance, refusing to leave until their loved ones were brought out of the mine. With the addition of rescue personnel, media crews, and volunteer workers, the encampment already held more than 400 people and continued growing by the hour.

The families had already staked out their own individual campsites, putting up small tents and building campfires. But larger canvas pavilions were being erected even as we arrived. The largest was a huge sky-blue pavilion such as are commonly raised for weddings or outdoor entertainment, which a nearby township had provided as a communal dining hall. Across the road from the family campsites, the media outlets were already moving in their campers and vans, even full-sized, air-conditioned mobile trailers. From their roofs sprouted satellite dishes and antennas. Beyond the encampment were the tall, metal cranes, drilling rigs, and other heavy equipment of the rescue operation.

As the other pastors and I walked through the camp, we spotted a number of uniformed police personnel. But they were far more involved in helping the camp residents than in carrying out their assigned mission of maintaining the peace. Though the mine catastrophe had been designated an official emergency, we saw no military personnel, a positive indicator of the lack of social tensions or violence such a disaster could easily have engendered.

What we did see was deep anguish. All around us people were weeping. Others rushed frantically here and there, expressions worried and preoccupied as they ferried supplies from one spot to another or carried out the various tasks assigned to them. The overall impression was of haste and anxiety. Mixed in with the multitude were news crews carrying out interviews and filming the scene. At this point, most of them were from Chile's own various media outlets.

But what drew the immediate attention of our party was the unhappy plight of the families awaiting news of their loved ones. Their small, cheap shelters were pitched on bare rock and sand. The thin material of the tents offered little relief from the fierce sun of the desert day and even less warmth against the chilly nights. Many of the families had traveled considerable distance to this mine where their menfolk worked. Some had come from Calera, on the coast 70 kilometers east. Others had arrived from the regional capital of Copiapó, where I lived, 50 kilometers southeast. Some had traveled from the mining port city of Chañaral, 160 kilometers northeast. There were even family members who'd made their way here from as far as Antofagasta, the Atacama Desert's largest municipality, more than 500 kilometers north of the mine.

Walking among the campsites, our group of pastors approached family members, inviting them to pray with us. No one refused our offer. We prayed to God with them for the essentials: courage, a positive spirit, strength to endure, hope. Above all we prayed for a miracle—the miracle of life.

"Heavenly Father, please keep the miners alive and safe," we prayed again and again.

We offered this prayer with unreserved confidence that God would respond. As pastors, we all knew from personal experience that God listens to the prayers of His children offered in faith. Over and over we repeated our plea for a miracle. From their participation, many of the family members too evidenced trust in God and were also believing in faith for a miracle.

We'd made a complete round of the camp when an idea came to my mind. I didn't pause to think it over but spoke up with immediate assurance that my idea was appropriate for the occasion. Turning to the others, I pointed toward a nearby knoll among the maze of hills and ridges surrounding the camp. "Look, just over there is a hill from which we'll be able to look out over the entire mine and encampment. What do you think if we climb up to the top together and from there pray to God as a group, asking Him to bring about a miracle for the miners?"

The other pastors expressed instant agreement. We climbed the hillside to its summit. From this position we could now see the dark, cavernous entrance to the mine not far ahead around a curve in the road that had blocked it from view at the encampment. Stretching away from us in every direction were rounded yellow hills, piles of sharp-edged rock slag, and a flat, beige expanse crisscrossed by ravines. Nowhere could we spot even a hint of vegetation. We were now deep in the Atacama Desert, the driest spot on earth, as wrinkled and crevassed and gray-brown as the stretched-out hide of a crocodile.

There at the summit of the hill, we raised our hands toward heaven and began to pray. "Heavenly Father, we need a miracle. No one knows here where the miners are or even if they are still alive. The weight of fallen rock is far too great to tunnel through. But we know Your power is even greater. Please keep these men alive. Guide the rescue crews to find them and to find them alive—all of them, that not a single one of them might be lost, Lord God."

Our prayers went on to include the family members, the rescue crews, anyone who might be carrying out any task to help save the miners. Our concern went well beyond just saving the lives of the trapped miners. This could not be otherwise. Each of us standing there on the hilltop was, after all, by vocation and calling, committed to bringing people to eternal salvation through Jesus Christ. We all wanted to see every person with whom we'd come into contact at Camp Hope experience the same joy of eternal life we'd found in Jesus Christ—an eternal life that does not begin in some distant future after death but right here and now with our life on this earth.

As we prayed, news crews mingling with family members and rescue personnel suddenly noticed our group standing on the hilltop with arms raised toward heaven. Approaching, they asked what we were doing. As journalists, they were always on the prowl for a good news story. In consequence, on the very next day, one of the regional newspapers included a front-page image of the fifteen pastors praying on top of the knoll.

From that moment, that particular hilltop began acquiring more and more symbolic importance for the rescue operation until in time it became the geographic focal point for the hopes of everyone there. Along its summit would be planted a semicircle of Chilean flags, one for each of the miners trapped below ground. Over the next weeks, press conferences and official announcements would be given there. From that hilltop, Chilean President Sebastian Piñera would eventually read the first message of hope from the trapped miners.

But that part of the story was still to come. At the time we knew nothing of what lay ahead. We didn't even know yet if there were thirty-four miners trapped below, as the news had been announcing, or thirty-three as the rumors were beginning to insist. We knew only that God had the power to answer our prayers. And so we prayed.

Coming back down from the hill into the camp, I noticed among the crowd a woman marching with a pole over one shoulder. The pole was no more than a stick she'd found somewhere. But fastened to one end of the stick hung a Chilean flag with its single white star on a background of blue, flanked by a stripe of white over a longer stripe of red. The woman, of average build and medium height, was not particularly out of the ordinary in appearance. But her stride was confident, her expression very determined. Though I took note of her, I had no idea then who she was.

As we made the return trip to Copiapó, I took time to reflect on our experiences at the mine. What I had seen that day had impacted me profoundly. I felt satisfied, if only partially, at what we'd been able to accomplish to this point. We had planted our flag on that hillside—the flag of prayer.

Back at home, I retreated into a preoccupied silence, my churning thoughts focused on one subject: the plight of the miners and their families. In light of such tragedy, that subject soon narrowed even further to become a single burning question: what should I do for these people?

The compulsion to act in some way weighed heavily on my heart, as though God were standing at my side, saying audibly to me, "You must do something to help."

But where would be a practical place to start? I'd seen that numerous tasks needed to be done, but there were few volunteers to do them. Up to this point only a few officials from nearby townships had shown up to offer aid. The encampment held at least 400 people, who would all need care. I'd even seen small children belonging to the trapped miners out there in that difficult environment.

I kept asking myself, *What to do? What to do?*

As I continued to mull over the question, one impulse kept thrusting itself to the surface. All those children staying at the camp needed immediate attention. And that attention I could at least provide without any further loss of time. What better distraction to cheer up unhappy children than by interacting with other youth like themselves? Throughout the churches under my supervision in Copiapó, we ran a wonderful children's program called the Pathfinder Club, similar to the Boy Scouts but providing also solid Bible teaching and strong Christian values. Among our teenage helpers in the clubs, I had a group of young people already organized and willing to jump into action. I called up the club leaders and made arrangements.

3

CHILDREN AND CHEERS

The next morning I drove out to the San José Mine encampment with a group of older Pathfinder Club members. Ranging from thirteen to sixteen years in age, these teenagers were already experienced in ministry with the younger children in the clubs.

Upon our arrival at Camp Hope, we learned that the latest news of the trapped miners was not encouraging. As the rescue teams had tried to clear a way in through the ventilation shaft, fresh avalanches, collapsing additional tunnels, had threatened their lives as well. Now this hopeful prospect for reaching the men was also sealed off.

The rescue teams had turned to a new tactic, using powerful percussion drills to bore a series of exploratory shafts about sixteen centimeters (six inches) in diameter. Their goal was to pierce through into the tunnel containing the emergency shelter, where it was hoped the miners had taken refuge, thereby reestablishing contact. Unfortunately, the maps available to the rescue crews of the mine's complex interior labyrinth were out of date. Nor at a depth of 700 meters (2300 feet) was it easy to pinpoint exactly where the tunnel lay in a direct line from the surface. To complicate matters further, the rock into which they were drilling was an unusually hard type of granite that made it extremely difficult to keep the drilling on a straight trajectory.

Even more discouraging, while equipment had been set up to listen for tapping, pounding, or other noises that might signal the miners were trying to communicate, to this point there had been no indication that any of the trapped men were still alive. A growing anxiety across Chile over the plight of the miners extended to the president of the republic himself. President Sebastian Piñera had made a surprise visit to the San José Mine the evening before to meet with coordinators of the rescue efforts as well as the families of the trapped miners.

When we arrived, the camp was abuzz with the news of the president's lightning visit. My own plans seemed paltry and trivial by comparison. Yet my young helpers and I carried on with our plans. First on our agenda was entertaining the children. These included sons and daughters, nieces and nephews, and even grandchildren of trapped miners. They numbered perhaps twenty in all, ranging in age from preschool up to twelve years old. We'd brought along some nutritious food items for them— milk, cereal, and other snacks.

We'd also brought reading material, a Christian children's magazine entitled *El Amigo de los Niños* (*The Friend of Children*), referring to Jesus Christ, who had once told his disciples, "Let the little children come to me" (Mark 10:14). The magazine was filled with entertaining stories, each of which reinforced some positive value such as hope, faith, courage, endurance, or prayer. For the adults we'd brought copies of another book, entitled *Señales de Esperanza* (*Signs of Hope*). This book offered biblical principles for coping with life's crises from a perspective of hope.

My youthful companions helped me distribute the food and literature. Then we gathered the camp children together, leading them in lively games and energetic action songs. It wasn't long before the children were shouting and laughing with delight. Their adult family members gathered around to watch. Until that moment there had only been tears, the only topic of conversation the tragedy of their loved ones, and the shared anguish over a complete lack of information. Did their husbands, sons, and brothers lie buried somewhere under that massive fall of rock? Were they injured and in pain? How many were still alive? The interminable suspense was agonizing.

But as such troubled thoughts were distracted by watching the children's noisy pleasure, we could see everyone's grief easing perceptibly. After the children's program ended, we again visited each family in turn, praying for them and for their loved ones trapped in the depths of the mine. The heartfelt prayers of my teenage helpers proved a special comfort to aching hearts, hope now taking the place of despair on their faces. As the hour came for us to return to Copiapó, all the families thanked us and begged us to return the next day.

That same day before heading back to Copiapó, I had my first encounter with the woman I'd seen the day before carrying the Chilean flag on a stick over her shoulder. This encounter took place not in person but on a large TV screen that had been set up so that residents of Camp Hope could follow the news coverage of their loved ones. There on the screen I recognized her: a round face bronzed by the sun, dark eyes, and an expression that was determined without being obstinate. The hands gripping her makeshift flagpole with its banner of red, white, and blue were strong and callused from hard work.

The woman was being interviewed by the press. Her voice was quiet and unhurried, showing no nervousness. The answers she gave to a flood of questions were shrewd, coherent, resolute. Responding to a question, she said firmly, "We came to this place when there was nothing here. Only the rocks beneath us. We barely slept. Our only beds were a few folding chairs."

As I listened, I found out that her name was María Segovia. A 48-year-old food vender known locally as "queen of the *empanada*" for the delicious fried meat and cheese pastries she sold at the city market, she was the sister of one of the missing miners, Dario Segovia. When María had received news of the disaster, she'd headed straight for San José Mine, demanding to know what had happened to her brother. Where was Dario? What were the mine owners doing to get him back? She didn't even ask whether he was alive or not. Her brother meant everything to her, and she was not even willing to consider that he might not be alive. When she could not get a satisfactory answer, María planted herself resolutely on a folding chair near the entrance, expressing her determination to wait there until her brother was brought out alive.

Other families soon began arriving as well. Since María was

already on the spot, she became the welcoming committee, greeting the newcomers with songs and chants to cheer them up. With María had come her brother Alberto, her sister Elizabeth, and Andrea, the wife of one of the other miners, Claudio Yañez. Together with them, she would lead the crowd in a chant, *"¡Los mineros de Chile!"* ("The miners of Chile!"), followed by a traditional national cheer that can be heard at any sporting event where the crowd is rooting for a Chilean victory: "Chi-chi-chi! Le-le-le! *¡Viva Chile!*" ("Long live Chile!").

These chants were repeated over and over, the entire group galvanized by María's enthusiasm. Because of her strength and fierce spirit, it wasn't long before María Segovia had been dubbed the "mayor of Camp Hope." In Chile, the title of mayor *(alcalde)* refers properly to the person who administrates a municipality, a person usually chosen by the community in a democratic general election. In Camp Hope there was no election, nor was María in any way in charge of administering the logistics and infrastructure of the camp. But in acknowledgement of her natural leadership, María became tacitly accepted as "mayor" of the trapped miner families through a process of general consent whose legitimacy no one questioned.

As the Pathfinder Club members and I visited family after family, praying with each that God would keep the miners alive, we arrived at the tent where María Segovia and her family were staying. I'd taken the time to find out which family lived in each tent, and I carried with me a list of the trapped individuals that had been published in one of the local newspapers. So I was able to ask María specifically, "Would you mind if we prayed with you for the safety of your brother Dario and the other miners?"

She responded instantly, "Any spiritual help is welcome here in the camp." She paused and then added, "We have faith that God is great and is going to bring our boys out of there."

Over the following days, I often spotted María working hard around the camp, and undoubtedly she noted me working there as well. But we did not come back into direct contact for another ten days.

Monday, August 9, was a school day. But the Pathfinder Club helpers I'd taken with me to Camp Hope were mostly students at Copiapó's Adventist school. The director of the school gave permission for my teenage assistants to miss classes, so on Monday morning I returned with them to San José Mine.

There had still been no sounds of life from the trapped miners. Discussions up at the camp were now revolving around the actions of the mayor of Caldera, the closest township to the mine where a number of the trapped miners lived. Since the San José Mine fell under her municipal jurisdiction, Mayor Brunilda González had called for an investigation into safety violations committed by the mine owners. By all accounts, these were multiple and continuing. In 2004 a miner had died in a cave-in. During 2006, a truck driver had been killed in an accident, and more than 180 other miners had been injured, more than fifty of them seriously.

In 2007 when a consulting geologist had been killed in an explosion, the Ministry of Mines finally ordered the mine shut down. But the mine had been reopened within the year without ever having improved the dangerous working conditions. On July 5, exactly a month before the current disaster, another miner had lost his leg after a slab of rock had fallen and crushed it. Although the mine owners had faced manslaughter charges because of some of the earlier incidents, they had always managed to get off by paying a few fines and meager compensation to the families.

Now family members were demanding that criminal charges be filed against the San Esteban Mining Company. Some were suggesting that the mine owners be forced to spend a day in jail for every day the miners spent underground. Mayor González had just ordered the seizure of paperwork and other documents pertinent to the case. Those heading up the investigation had announced their determination to bring to account those responsible for the tragedy. The question was, who had authorized the reopening of the mine and under what circumstances? Whatever answer emerged would greatly affect the owners of the mine and perhaps even officials of Chilean government agencies.

In this tense atmosphere, my teenage assistants and I began our own planned activities for the day. This time we added practical service projects and prayer time to the recreation with the children. We gathered wood for campfires, an urgent need with the desert's cold nights. We helped dish up food in the dining tent. We raised two large banners that read, "Let us continue praying for the miners."

These were nothing fancy, just simple phrases lettered on a plain canvas backdrop. But they offered a point of focus for the camp residents to think of their trapped loved ones, not just with worry and anguish, but with the hope and comfort that come through a trusting communication with a loving, caring heavenly Father. Those two banners remained in place until the very end of the rescue operation.

I found it interesting how quickly the focus at the camp could change from the urgent practical needs of the situation to emotions. This was certainly due in large measure to the media teams, who were eager to relay those emotions to a watching world outside Camp Hope. They wrote up news reports and aired video footage of the Pathfinder Club members playing with the camp children. The affectionate compassion demonstrated by these young volunteers had a positive impact on the entire camp. Just watching the children playing happily where such a short time before they had been in tears proved a powerful emotional therapy for their adult relatives. It seemed to give them renewed hope and confidence, an antidote to the pain and anguish everyone was feeling.

The news commentary continued to debate the exact number of trapped miners. Some still insisted there were thirty-four. This was the actual number scheduled to be down there on that afternoon. Others insisted there were only thirty-three, because one of the scheduled miners had not shown up to work that day. Each time the newspapers published the list of those miners confirmed missing, one additional victim would be listed: "NN, whose identity we are still seeking to establish."

4

GOD WORKS THROUGH
SIMPLE MEANS

Finishing the activities of that day, my youthful helpers and I returned home. That night I found myself unable to sleep, in a turmoil of conflicting emotions. What we had accomplished thus far had been good but not nearly enough. We needed to do more to help the families, not just the children. These family members were desperate to see their loved ones out of the mine, free from danger, healthy, and safe.

The incessant waiting, brief though it had been so far, was excruciating. A third day had gone by without any news. Then a fourth day. Again nothing. Anguish had become a permanent state for the family members, each day stronger, more painful, harder to endure. I wanted to do something more, something effective—something that would make an immediate difference to these people.

I lay there in bed, thinking about the residents of Camp Hope. Up to this point, we'd concerned ourselves with their daily physical needs: food, water, shade against the day's heat, warm coverings against the cold nights. But beyond all that was the loneliness and isolation each family was undergoing. It was a peculiar loneliness, considering that they were all living in such close quarters, eating, talking, passing the time together like one large extended family. Still, each family's personal loss was unique. Only one thought occupied their minds: the injustice of what had happened to the miners. The conversations I'd overheard never varied. Everyone felt the same anger, the same uncertainty, the same anguish.

"Aren't you going to sleep?" my wife, Gloria, asked me. "Sleep, rest! You need to rest."

"It's that I can't stop thinking of the miners and their families," I answered her. "What can be done for them? Those men are buried at such a terrible depth—if any of them are still alive!— maybe trapped in some tiny space without food or water. We hope and pray they are still alive. But if they are, how must they be feeling right now? What must their psychological state be? They would have to be feeling desperately depressed and alone down there, wondering if anyone is even trying to rescue them. It would be easy under such terrible circumstances to just give up hope, to stop even trying to stay alive."

I continued thinking about the miners and about their families, not only those at Camp Hope, but other family members waiting anxiously for news back in their own homes all over Chile. It was already clear that whatever happened to the trapped miners would deeply affect the entire nation. Only rarely do events converge to bring together the population of a country in complete unity and closeness. In this past year, Chile had already had the unusual opportunity to live through several such unifying experiences.

The first had been the terrible earthquake that occurred around 3:30 a.m. local time on February 27, 2010. The quake's epicenter had been just offshore of Chile's Pacific coastline, not far from where I myself had grown up. Its magnitude of 8.8 on the Richter scale made it the second strongest earthquake registered in the history of Chile and the fifth strongest recorded worldwide since 1900, far more powerful than the earthquake that had devastated Haiti only a few weeks earlier on January 12. The earthquake itself had been followed by an equally devastating tsunami wave. Thanks to Chile's stricter building codes, the loss of life was considerably less severe than Haiti had suffered, less than a thousand deaths in all. But the devastation had displaced at least 1.5 million Chileans from their homes. Stunned by the sheer immensity of the destruction, the entire nation had pulled together to tackle the arduous task of rebuilding. By the time of the San José Mine disaster six months after the earthquake, the reconstruction process was well underway.

The other significant experiences unifying the nation were far more pleasant in nature. The year 2010 marked the bicentennial celebration of Chile's existence as an independent nation. The actual anniversary would be celebrated on September 18, but a number of celebratory activities were planned throughout the year. Then there was the qualification of Chile's national soccer team for the World Cup finals. For both of these, the habitual cheerful enthusiasm for which the Chilean people were famed had brought together the entire population in a unified expression of joy and fierce national pride.

Now once again the nation had been united. And once again, it was because of a tragedy. Mining was Chile's biggest industry, part of the national identity. All over the country, the Chilean people were not just talking about the disgraceful scandal of what had happened at San José Mine; they were living it with the trapped miners, suffering together with these men and their families. The massive media coverage made it possible for the entire population to participate with each new turn of events at the mine, even while they went about their own daily activities.

I was well aware of the national identity these miners represented. But I had not yet realized that any specific help we might offer to them and to their families would also have to extend in some degree to the entire nation. In truth, the meagerness of all our efforts to this point compared to the sheer magnitude of the disaster made it difficult for me to even begin to grasp any truly nationwide perspective. Surely no pastor of a small regional district with an extremely limited congregation could possibly make a real difference to all these miners and their families, to say nothing of an entire country.

So as I pleaded with God on that sleepless night for His intervention, it had not yet so much as entered my thoughts that I might ask God to include the entire nation of Chile in that plea. But God knows our hearts, and He answers our prayers according to His own divine standards: abundantly above what we ask or think when our asking is small; less than our anxious entreaties when, because of our own distress, we make demands beyond what is really required to meet our needs.

As I finished my urgent conversation with God, one idea took hold in my mind. *A Bible for each of the families! That is what I will do tomorrow. They have nothing to occupy their time and thoughts up there at the camp during the day. Regardless of how the rescue operation transpires, their wait will be a long one. They need to concentrate their thoughts on something greater than their own anguish, something healthier than their own pain. What better solution than a Bible for each family?*

Even as I made that decision, I continued to pray for a miracle on behalf of the miners. All Chile was doing the same, as was a very large part of the planet's population.

5

A GIFT OF HOPE

By the next day, August 10, things had become even more complicated up at San José Mine. After his fleeting visit to the mine, it seemed to me that President Sebastian Piñera had been left facing two difficult realities.

The first was the situation of the trapped miners. The only realistic option was to admit publicly that things were not going well. At best, their rescue would be extremely difficult, the final outcome not in the hands of any government but of the Almighty Himself. At the same time, a decision had to be made whether to commit the full resources of the Chilean government to the rescue operation, regardless of the expense involved. It was already clear that the San Esteban Mining Company, which operated San José Mine, had neither the ability nor the necessary equipment to carry out a rescue.

The second reality was discontent and grumbling among the families of the trapped miners. On his brief visit to Camp Hope the president had not taken time to meet with every family, focusing instead on discussions with rescue personnel and mining officials. President Piñera made every effort to explain his actions. But far more gratifying to the families was a firm public commitment to saving the miners.

"I personally promised the families of the trapped miners," he announced in a press conference, "that the rescue operations will continue with all the strength in the world."

It was a commitment from which neither President Piñera nor the Chilean government wavered in the weeks ahead. From then on, the president also always made a point of meeting with the Camp Hope family members before anyone else, including even the media, taking careful note of their opinions and wishes.

By this time it had already become clear that if the miners were found alive, rescuing them from more than a half-kilometer below the surface was going to be more challenging and costly than had ever been expected. President Piñera made an appeal to the international community for help, especially the United States, Canada, and Australia, all countries with highly developed mining industries.

"If there is any technology out there, any knowledge that will help us," the Chilean president pleaded simply, "we will use it."

The investigation set in motion by Mayor Brunilda González of Caldera had already borne fruit as the Chilean authorities announced the removal from office of Alejandro Vio, director of the National Service of Geology and Mines. His authorization had permitted the operators to reopen the San José Mine without taking the necessary steps to comply with safety regulations. Concerned to avoid criminal charges and fines, the San Esteban Company owners, Marcelo Kemeny and Alejandro Bohn, were already insisting that none of this was any fault of theirs. They'd complied with necessary safety procedures. If there were tunnel collapses, then the miners themselves were clearly not doing their jobs properly. In any case, the miners were well aware of the risks they were taking in accepting a job at San José Mine.

The owners continued to insist as well that the miners were all still alive, though they could offer no such evidence. With San José Mine's past record of safety violations and injuries, the families of the trapped miners were furious at their statements. The excuses coming from mine owners did nothing to help their case but merely made the San Esteban Mining Company look even worse in the eyes of the Chilean people and a watching world.

By this time the government had appointed a mining engineer, André Sougarret, the general manager of El Teniente—the world's largest underground mine, owned by Chile's state-owned copper corporation, Codelco—to spearhead the rescue operation. Rescue crews were now working around the clock, drilling nine different boreholes down to where they hoped to intersect with the tunnel where the refuge was located. But to this point there'd been no success, and hope was fading for a positive outcome. In fact, on Thursday, August 12, exactly one week after the mine collapse, Minister of Mines Laurence Golborne made a grim public announcement that the likelihood of finding the miners still alive was now extremely slim. By Friday, August 13, one of the probes reached a depth of over 500 meters, offering a dim ray of hope, though still no concrete signs of life had turned up.

On Sunday, August 15, the miner families informally christened their makeshift township of tents, mobile trailers, police
outposts, sheds and pavilions belonging to the rescue operation,
and wooden observation platforms constructed by various media
crews. The name they chose was *Campamento Esperanza*, or Camp
Hope, to affirm their faith in an ultimate rescue of the miners.

The huge sky-blue pavilion donated to the camp was the
focal point of daily life. The southern half had been designated a
dining hall; the northern half was offered as shelter under which
the families could stake out their own individual tents. Gradually,
from that first day until the actual rescue of the miners, more and
more family members relocated to the mine, since most lived too
far to return every day to their homes, whether in distant cities or
closer communities.

The main entrance of the mine was some fifty to seventy
meters north of the big tent. The rear of the tent backed onto a
hillside, the same hillside on which I and the rest of the fifteen
evangelical pastors had gathered to pray. By this time, a semicircle
of Chilean flags, each representing one of the thirty-three miners,
had been planted on top of the hill. By planting them where we
had prayed, the flags offered the additional symbolism of representing the many prayers going up for each miner. A much larger
banner displayed the faces of all the miners, their photos provided
by family members.

The space provided underneath the big pavilion for the small
family tents was not nearly big enough. Some families moved
their transitory shelters to a spot outside the dining tent to the
southeast. Volunteers from surrounding towns contributed firewood to the camp, essential against the nighttime cold, which

was intense here in the desert, especially now in August, which for our country south of the equator was the middle of winter. The firewood was dumped among those small tents southeast of the dining pavilion. Each family would take for themselves enough to build a campfire in front of their tent each evening.

During the day, in contrast, the sun offered intense heat. But without moisture in the atmosphere to retain that heat, by 6 p.m., when the sun had dropped behind the mountain peaks, a chill invaded the camp so bitter it seemed to turn one's very bones to ice. At that time of evening, with the campfires providing light and heat and a hot drink to accompany the supper rations, there was finally leisure to relax from the day's busy activity and engage in casual conversation about the latest camp happenings and news updates. This conversation was always sad, always anxious, but at the same time always tinged with an element of hope. Hence the name chosen: Camp Hope.

The news crews often expressed how impressed they were with the atmosphere of unity and affection within the camp. The usual elements that so often divided the Chilean people—political, religious, social, and economic differences, even sports rivalries—had been laid aside, at least within the camp boundary. What remained was a common commitment to help these suffering families and a common hope to see the trapped miners out of the mine and out of danger. It was eminently satisfying to see journalists sitting down for a plain cooked plate of rice in the modest shelter of a mining family, to watch senators and congressmen conversing with simple laborers without the usual ulterior motives of seeking votes, to witness mining executives mixing with rescue crews as brothers. At least for this moment, everyone at the camp was an equal.

The same occurred with the food and supplies. The news crews had arranged for lodging back in the city, but Copiapó was a good fifty kilometers from the mine. They couldn't take a run back there just for a meal. So they would approach where they could see food being cooked, asking, "*¿Cuánto vale?* How much?"

The Camp Hope resident would respond, "Nothing. Just serve yourself. Everything here is free for everyone."

When journalists were thirsty, they would walk up to the cold drinks stand and ask, "How much is a soda?"

The answer they received was the same: "Don't worry, it's all free."

The general dining tent too was open to all comers, thanks to the generosity of many area businesses, supermarkets, churches, and individuals who donated food supplies to the camp residents and rescue personnel. Even the police officials assigned to the camp demonstrated the same attitude of solidarity and neighborly concern. Yes, they were there as security forces to maintain order if required. But for now, they helped carry firewood, played soccer with the children, or pitched in at whatever task a nearby person might be undertaking. They were friendly, smiling, kind, always respectful to the camp residents.

The same spirit characterizing Camp Hope at its beginning continued all the way to the end of what turned out to be a long wait for rescue. But if Camp Hope lived up to its name, that spirit of hope and unity did not exempt its residents from suffering. In fact suffering was its principal component, the conflict between hope and anguish always waiting to pounce. At times that suffering took on a life of its own, and all else in the camp seemed to succumb to its onslaught.

By now new rockslides inside the mine were hindering rescue efforts. Worries were growing that even if the miners were still alive, continued drilling might set off additional cave-ins right where the miners were supposed to be, burying them alive. But there was no alternative, and the drilling crews continued their work. By August 18, the probes had reached a depth of 600 meters.

In the meantime, since the ventilation shaft through which rescue crews had hoped to reach the miners had collapsed, other crews had been trying to dig out the collapsed tunnel by way of the main entrance ramp. But they had advanced through the debris only two kilometers when they ran into a wall of solid granite. This was the huge chunk of mountain that had "sat" on the mine. Weighing well upwards of a half-million tons, it could not be blasted away or dug through. Now with every other exit blocked, even if rescue crews made contact with the miners, how could they ever get them out? Besides, any supplies available to the miners would have long since been exhausted. What likelihood was there now that any would still be alive?

The news of this fresh setback triggered renewed despondency and anguish. The general atmosphere in the camp—as much among government personnel and rescue crews, even the media crews, as among the miners' own families—was escalating frustration and helplessness.

It was into this depressing environment that I arrived Thursday morning, August 19, with the Bibles I'd brought for each of the trapped miners' families. In my preoccupation to assemble enough Bibles and get them out to the camp, I hadn't even taken note that this afternoon at 2:00 would mark exactly two weeks since the mine collapse. Setting up a simple display on a table, I laid out the Bibles. Then I called for each family group in turn, following the order in which their campsites were staked out across the camp. Inside the cover of each Bible, I'd written out a personalized dedication that included the name of the missing miner and his family: for example, "Franklin Lobos and family."

Holding up one of the Bibles, I spoke to the entire group. "This Bible is a very special gift in which you can find hope, faith, strength, and salvation to sustain you in this very difficult time through which you are now living."

To each family as I handed them the Bible, I added simply, "I would like to offer you this Bible as a gift to strengthen and encourage you as the search goes on for your loved ones."

Then I prayed with each family in turn. In my prayer, I asked God to give them strength and courage, to bless the efforts of the government and the rescue teams, even the drills and other equipment, so that there might soon be a positive outcome in the search for the miners.

I spent that entire morning and part of the afternoon handing out the Bibles. I did not manage to complete my task because at 2:00 p.m. an earsplitting blast of a truck horn reverberated through the camp. Then all the vehicles at the mine site began honking their horns simultaneously, commemorating the two weeks that had now passed since the rockslide had trapped the miners. There was no organized memorial ceremony to mark the occasion, only that deafening and repetitive tribute to the terrible moment of the catastrophe. After all, there was nothing to celebrate and much to lament. Yet it was unknown whether the miners might still be clinging to life down below or were already dead and buried under the rubble.

The boreholes being drilled by the rescue teams were angled to break through into one of the lower-level tunnels or chambers near the emergency shelter where it was hoped the miners might have taken refuge. The percussion drill that had taken the lead had during the last twenty-four hours advanced another 120 meters. This should have been very good news, but it wasn't. They had now reached 720 meters, deeper than the level at which the miners should have taken refuge, without having made any contact. The probe had failed. An examination made it clear that the borehole had deviated from its target by a full ten meters.

Standing at a microphone, his voice unsteady, Minister of Mines Laurence Golborne made the announcement. The reaction of the camp residents was furious, almost violent. The Chilean police force had to form a circle around the minister to protect him from the jostling crowd. Despite their protective shield, the miner families confronted him vehemently, demanding that they be given the full truth about the situation.

"I am truly sorry," Laurence Golborne responded gently. "My heart is aching with all of you over this situation. We will continue to make every effort to find these men and then retrieve them from the mine. I am not asking you to be happy about this, because the news, as I've already told you, isn't good. None of us have any idea of what is going on down there or what is going to happen."

It was a moment of deep grief for all. The family members of the trapped miners were inconsolable. Everyone in Camp Hope suffered together—and not just in the camp. The entire country of Chile was saddened and disheartened at this new turn of events.

6

FAITH UNDER PRESSURE

Though once again attempts at contact with the miners had failed, the words President Sebastian Piñera had shared that very morning in a press conference were still worth following.

"Let us keep alive our hope," he declared, "because we have every reason to believe that in the zone where the miners were trapped, there is adequate oxygen and water, which are the vital elements necessary for their survival."

In a later press interview, engineer André Sougarret, who had coordinated the San José Mine rescue, was asked, "What was your moment of greatest despair during the rescue operation?"

He responded, "August 19, still four days before we knew whether or not any of the thirty-three were still alive, when we finally reached a depth beyond our goal of 700 meters and we discovered we'd completely missed the mark. It was extremely discouraging because we had now reached the lowest level of the mine without having yet made any contact with the miners. The waiting families began losing patience and demanding another alternative. They were insisting we allow *pirquineros*"—independent miners using pickaxes—"into the mine to try digging out the trapped men, not at all a practical solution. And yet we ourselves had logically always had doubts that we could drill down that far and effectively hit a space so narrow with a probe that small in diameter."

In giving the interview, André Sougarret did not describe the anguish of the camp residents, but it was great. The hope invested in that probe had been tremendous. Its failure was equally distressing. The families had spent all that night and the next morning in eager expectation. They'd all known that the drill was scheduled to break through near the emergency shelter where it was supposed the miners had taken refuge. Then came the bad news: the probe had failed. All over the camp, people were weeping, families holding each other close, grief-stricken and in despair. It seemed that all the hope they'd clung to had now died within them.

At that moment we had no idea, of course, what was happening down in the mine itself. But as we came to learn later, that same despair and anguish was multiplied among the miners themselves. They'd heard the noise of the drill descending toward them. They could judge from the sound just how far away it was from where they were gathered. It was very close. Then closer yet. They began to celebrate its imminent arrival.

Then to their horror and dismay, they heard the drill pass down to a deeper level. It had missed them. Then once again the silence, that disastrous silence, the same awful silence they'd been experiencing all these days. After that attempt, as the miners shared later, they were convinced the rescue team would abandon the search. Surely by now they would be convinced that the miners were all dead.

Far above, the families had gathered in one big group. No one had called for an assembly. But their shared pain had stirred up among the camp residents a need for mutual support. Such support as could be found only with others undergoing the same anguish. And so they came together. They wept together, talked anxiously about the failure of the probe, shared their frustration and sadness over the terrible news.

Then, raggedly at first, with patent apathy, the multitude began to raise their usual cheers. As one family after another joined in, they shouted out defiantly that traditional Chilean battle cry: "¡Chi, Chi, Chi! ¡Le, Le, Le! Chile! ¡Sí se puede! [Yes, we can!] ¡Viva, Chile!"

Their chanting held none of the joyous enthusiasm such a cheer usually generates in the Chilean people. Tears poured down their faces even as they shouted the words, their expressions distraught. My heart ached with them. The noisy honking to commemorate two weeks since the mine collapse, followed by the bad news of the failed probe, had kept me from delivering all the Bibles. Three still remained to be handed out. Picking up one of them, I approached the gathered multitude.

My purpose was simply to demonstrate solidarity by standing with them, to come alongside them in their pain. The nearest family group was huddled together, and I heard one of them say to another, "Look, maybe you could recite the Lord's prayer."

Immediately, I turned to a family member standing close to me. "I am a pastor. I would be glad to offer a prayer."

Without hesitation, the family member spoke up. "We have a pastor here. He can pray."

Suddenly, media teams surrounded the group. Before I could do anything, one of them said to me, "Pastor, would you please move over here a little so that we can all focus our cameras."

I shifted position as they requested and then turned my attention back to the group of weeping families. Raising the Bible I'd brought, I began to speak. "Dear friends, God gave us His Word as a gift, so that we might receive strength and hope. Right now we are going to pray together for a miracle."

I raised my own silent prayer heavenward, asking God to give me the right words. Then I prayed aloud, "Lord, please strengthen these families in this time of trial. Give them endurance, hope, faith. We plead as well for a miracle. Please watch over all thirty-three miners, that they may still be found alive. In the name of Jesus. Amen."

When I finished praying, we recited together the Lord's Prayer. Already I noted in the atmosphere a lessening of their anguished despair, an air of renewed hope radiating outward through the crowd. The horns had at last ceased their honking. The desert stretching away all around us seemed to settle into its own vast, empty silence. With the ending of our prayers, the families themselves had fallen into a reverent silence.

Into that silence, I announced, "I am here today giving out Bibles. I have a copy here signed to each family. If any family still has not received theirs, please just come to this table, and I will be glad to give you one."

As I finished giving out the Bibles, I shared a brief conversation with one of the recipients, Angélica Álvarez, married to one of the trapped miners, Edison Peña. Tears streaming down her cheeks as she accepted the Bible, she told me, "Pastor, I am so unhappy, so distressed. But you know what, I believe that God has a purpose in all that is happening."

I was deeply touched by her clear faith and spiritual understanding despite the terrible tragedy in which she found herself. Yes, God certainly does have a purpose, I agreed with her.

Angélica went on, "Despite all my grief, despite all my pain, despite the fact that we still have not found the men or had any news of them, I believe that God has a great plan in all this."

Then she added, "The great plan that God has is that we turn our hearts fully back to Him, because up to this point we have all been so guilty of seeking after God only when we find ourselves in trouble."

Just a week earlier, Angélica had written out a message to her husband on a large boulder near her tent. Months later, when the rescue was all over, that message could still be seen on that boulder, its words still clearly legible: "Edison, we are making every effort to get you out. Both technical and human resources are working day and night so that all will turn out well and all of you can return to your families. May God direct this great work. August 11, 2010."

I prayed with her, for her, and for all of the thirty-three miners. From that moment we worked together frequently to organize different activities on behalf of the families. Angélica was already an influential leader among the group, and her influence continued to grow.

It was well past dark by the time I headed home that night to Copiapó. My emotions were again mixed. I felt a certain relief that the Bibles were now all in the hands of the families where they could be a source of the spiritual comfort and hope they needed now more than ever. At the same time I felt disheartened, because the failure of the probe had left everyone in continued ignorance as to the fate of the miners. To my despondency was added a mounting frustration.

The night was now very black around me as I drove carefully along the narrow, winding curves toward the city. My churning thoughts felt as jolting as the bumpy asphalt ribbon under my tires, as black as the night around me, as chilled and gloomy as a rainy day. In this darkness, I couldn't see the desert around me, but I could feel its parched emptiness without trees, grass, plants, flowers—without anything. The bleak aridity of this driest spot on the planet seemed to invade everything around me, including my own mind and spirit. Only the twin yellow beams of my headlights offered a faint illumination to brighten the dark road ahead.

I prayed, "Without Your light, Lord, what would we do? Help us see beyond this current failure. I know You control all things, that with Your power You can do anything. You are capable of bringing about this miracle that we have pleaded for so many times. May Your powerful hand protect and care for each of these families, that they may come to believe in You. May all these miners, their children, and their relatives also come to believe in You. And not just them, but all the people of Chile, and all the nations of the world."

The next day I had a new thought. The Gypsy congregation that was under my pastoral supervision had been praying for the miners. The group gathered four times a week in their *kanyiri*, as it was called in Romany, actually a big tent they used as a church. In each of their gatherings, they'd been praying for the miners. Several times they'd expressed their desire to go up to Camp Hope to pray onsite for the miners.

They would say to me, "Pastor, *Odel sibaró*"—which means that God is great and powerful. "He can do this miracle."

These Gypsy Christians express their faith in God with such conviction and contagious joy that I knew they could give the miner families the spiritual refreshment they desperately needed in this critical hour. It was time to take them up on their offer to visit the camp. We made arrangements for a group from the Gypsy congregation to travel to Camp Hope the next day, Saturday. I couldn't go with them as that day I had a prior commitment in the town of Chañaral, a full 200 kilometers from Copiapó. Nor could the main leader of the Gypsy church, Ramón Curín, who was a paramedic at Copiapó's central hospital and one of the three paramedics who had been taking turns providing medical care to the residents of Camp Hope.

But I arranged with a number of other leaders to accompany the Gypsy group. Among them were Julio Meléndez, the patriarch of all the Gypsies in that region, and Mario Betancur, a strong, faithful Christian who shared the leadership of the Gypsy congregation with Ramón Curín. Ramón himself is part Mapuche, Chile's largest indigenous Indian group, a direct descendent from Lautaro and Caupolicán, two legendary heroes of the tribe. Like his Mapuche ancestors, he is creative, efficient, and very much a leader. Another who joined them was Fernando Pinto, a volunteer lay leader whose wife, Carolina Poblete, oversees a school for Gypsy children.

So they went. Fernando Pinto shared with me later how their trip had gone. The Gypsies had visited the families, handed out 100 copies of the book *Signs of Hope*, read the Bible with various families, prayed, and shared their beautiful Romany praise music with the whole camp. Their soloist Yanko had sung several special numbers. The camp residents had expressed their appreciation, applauding the Romany music enthusiastically. The contagious joy of the Gypsy Christians' faith in God caught the attention of the media crews, and the Chilean National Television channel extensively covered their visit to Camp Hope.

Having finished with my own commitment in Chañaral, I stopped by Camp Hope. Night had fallen, and the campfires were now burning. As I walked through the campsites staked out by the different families, I came to the tent of María Segovia, the camp "mayor." Sitting outside around the fire with María were a group of family members and friends. As usual, the night was bitterly cold, and the flames flickering skyward from their small fire had little effect against the darkness.

I stopped to talk. María as always was the center of attention. Every person around the campfire as they spoke directed their conversation towards her. It was a pleasure to witness the growing leadership of this woman, always so dynamic and hardworking in anything that needed to be done but demonstrating as well a deep spiritual sensitivity and closeness to God. She reminded me of some valiant warrior who had stepped right off the pages of Scripture to fight on behalf of the miners and their families. Or perhaps she was more like some valiant warrior of the mines who stepped into the pages of Scripture to energize herself with the power of God's Word, returning to the daily routine of the rescue operation with even greater strength and confidence.

I paused briefly beside the Segovias' campfire to wish them good night. Looking around at the entire group, I said, "*Que Dios les bendiga*. May God bless you. Tomorrow in all our churches, we will continue to pray that the thirty-three miners will be found and that they will all be alive and well." Receiving my comments as though directed to her personally, María offered a regal nod and thanked me for the prayers.

7

ALIVE!

Meanwhile the other drilling probes had continued their work. At midmorning on Sunday, August 22, I was at home in Copiapó with my wife Gloria. Suddenly we heard the sound of car horns blaring from every direction.

"Can it be they've found the miners?" I said to my wife.

"I wouldn't think so," she responded. "Let's turn on the TV."

The television news contained two important pieces of information. The rescue crews had heard what appeared to be intentional noises coming from the depths of the mine. And the president of Chile would be arriving at the mine within the next half hour.

"Then they must be alive," I told my wife. "But they don't want to make the announcement until the president arrives. If it weren't so, why would he come? And what else could those noises be?"

Just then the news commentator announced that according to some experts the noises could just be some rocks that had fallen, striking against the metal of the drill probe. I turned to my wife. "Gloria, I'm going to the mine."

"Go immediately," she responded.

I snatched up my knapsack. As I headed out the door, she called after me, "How are you going to get to the mine?"

In one of my recent trips to the mine, my radiator had sprung a leak. I'd had to have it towed the final stretch to the city. At this very moment, the vehicle was in the mechanic's shop, scheduled for repair.

"I don't know," I answered.

Accustomed to seeing in Scripture how God always resolved the problems of His followers as a normal aspect of their daily lives, I added, "God will provide."

I walked out to the main road that leads from Copiapó toward Caldera, the nearest municipality to San José Mine. With the mine a good fifty kilometers away, my plan was to hitch a ride. The one difficulty was that there were three police checkpoints along the road. Today with the president arriving at the mine, the checkpoint guards were bound to be more stringent than usual.

This particular road didn't have much traffic. I'd walked along the highway perhaps ten kilometers when a vehicle overtook me heading the same direction. I flagged it down. As the vehicle pulled up beside me, I could see a man and a woman inside. They were a married couple, I soon discovered as we chatted.

"Are you headed up to the San José Mine?" I asked them.

"Yes," they answered. "Climb in."

As I did so, I could hear a local radio station playing. On it, a newscaster was repeating the news. "They have heard noises down in the depths of the mine."

I could still hear the blaring of car and truck horns expressing excitement at the news—or rather at renewed hope, since the news was still indefinite and uncertain. Gesturing toward the radio, the wife commented to her husband, "You see, I told you, God does exist."

He smiled but did not say a word as he continued driving.

Tears pouring down her cheeks, his wife repeated, "You see that God does exist. I told you that God exists."

We began conversing on the subject. I gave the couple a Bible I had with me, just like the ones I'd given the miner families. Through these kind people and their vehicle, God had quickly supplied my transport. But as we reached the first police checkpoint, a second difficulty arose. This time the difficulty extended to my companions as well. At the checkpoint, an armed police guard waved us to a stop. As I'd anticipated, the presence of President Piñera up at the mine had prompted extra restrictions, since there'd been no such difficulties on my earlier visits to the mine. Something special was going on up there, and the police were evidently trying to prevent a mob of strangers unconnected to San José Mine or Camp Hope from swarming the place.

"Can we pass?" the husband of the couple asked.

"No!" the checkpoint guard answered bluntly.

Sometime earlier at the beginning of the San José Mine crisis, Chile's Adventist radio station, Radio Nuevo Tiempo, or New Times Radio, had issued me press credentials to serve as their representative at the mine, from where I would report from time to time with a summary of what was happening for their news service. Now I pulled out my press pass and showed it to the guard.

"Okay, yes, you can pass," he responded.

During the next part of the trip, I shared with the couple about my faith in God, His existence and power to bring about miracles, His compassion in responding to our prayers, and all that God does for the human beings He has created. Then we arrived at the second checkpoint. A new difficulty.

"You cannot pass," the checkpoint guard announced.

I showed him my press credentials. "I am with Radio Nuevo Tiempo."

"Do you have credentials endorsed by the authorities of the camp?" he demanded.

"No, I don't," I admitted.

"Then you cannot go any farther," he responded firmly.

That was as far as my kindly chauffeurs were able to go. Climbing out of the car to speak with another checkpoint guard, I showed him my press credentials from Radio Nuevo Tiempo. In contrast to his companion, he immediately said, "Yes, of course you can enter. Go on through. But that vehicle can't go any farther."

Now I was once again without transport. Camp Hope was still another two kilometers up the road. But just as I began walking, a vehicle filled with rescue personnel pulled up to the checkpoint. They invited me to ride up to the camp with them. Once again God had resolved my problem. The third checkpoint, just outside the mine, offered no difficulties at all. They didn't even wave the rescue vehicle to a stop.

When we arrived at the camp, the helicopter bearing the president was just settling down for a landing. As soon as President Piñera exited the helicopter, he headed for the hillside where the flags representing the thirty-three miners were waving in the wind beyond the dining tent. While media crews and camp residents crowded around, he pulled out a piece of paper that had been sealed in a clear, plastic bag. The paper was small, with uneven borders that had been torn by hand, the paper itself discolored from damp and dirt. It carried a message from the very depths of the mine, the president announced.

Yes, it was true. That very morning, Sunday, August 22, contact had at last been reestablished with the trapped miners. A probe had broken through a tunnel roof. When it was pulled out, the first evidence of contact immediately spotted by rescue crews was fresh red paint that had been smeared as a signal across the tip of the drill. Then they had discovered this paper taped to the drill's base. Scrawled across it in what looked also to be red marker or paint was a message.

His voice choked with emotion, President Piñera read the message. "We are all alive and well in the refuge, all 33."

They were alive! Not just some of the miners, but all of them! The miracle we'd prayed for had occurred. Just as Thursday, August 19, only three days earlier, had been viewed as a day of failure and despair, so August 22 was now hailed as a day of life, of rejoicing, of celebration.

It was now 2:00 in the afternoon. The good news raced like a brush fire across Chile even as the televised images flashed around the entire world. Everywhere people were laughing, crying, jumping up and down, hugging each other, dancing in the streets.

Those who'd been involved in the drama of that day acknowledged that this truly was a miracle. A few weeks later on October 17, the prestigious Chilean newspaper, *El Mercurio*, conducted an

extensive press interview with engineer André Sougarret, who'd
headed up the San José rescue operation. Among the many questions asked, several related to the events of August 22.

"Are you a believer?"

"Yes, I am a believer."

"Did you pray during these past months?"

"Many times, especially in connection to my own puzzlement
over why certain things happened as they did. Why certain situa-
tions turned out in a way that really had no logical explanation."

"To what are you referring?"

"With the probes we were sending down, things happened
that just didn't make sense from an engineering standpoint. I
believe with all my heart that something beyond just the physical
happened down there."

"Is the head of rescue operations insinuating this was a miracle?"

"I'm speaking of the most incredible good luck. I wouldn't
go so far as to call it a miracle, because the truth is that we were
completely prepared ahead of time for exactly what ended up happening. But here is an example. We would send down the probe
expecting it to head a certain direction, and it would end up drifting off course at a very different angle, but one that ended up
benefiting our operation. That is precisely what happened with
the final probe, which ended up becoming our Plan B. We didn't
have much hope that we would reach the tunnel where the men
were, but it ended up breaking through exactly at the right spot.
We needed the angle to straighten out and make a course correc-
tion at the very bottom of our borehole where drilling is at the
most difficult. And it did so, breaking through at the very corner
of the chamber where the men were. We're talking centimeters

here. A few centimeters difference, and we'd never have broken through. We certainly had incredible good luck. Or help!"

"Help from who? From God?"

"Well, there certainly have been some things … all those numbers even, I really couldn't say."

"You believe in all these coincidences then about the number 33?"

"I have no logical explanation. But all the world has been asking, why those numbers. Something helped out here. Faith, maybe. Prayer. The focused desire of the entire world that we would succeed."

In asking about the number 33, the journalist was referring to a popular speculation circulating widely around Chile that gave special significance to the number 33. The drilling of the rescue shaft had taken 33 days. The shaft itself was 66 centimeters across, or 33 times 2. The note sent up with a message that all 33 miners were still alive contained 33 characters, including spaces between words. The final rescue itself began on 13/10/10 (October 13, 2010, as written in Latin America, where the date comes before the month), numerals which added up to 33. Besides which it was quickly pointed out that according to Scripture Jesus Christ was 33 years old when he was crucified and rose again.

By the date of that interview with André Sougarret, it had become amply evident to both the trapped miners and those on the surface that throughout the entire process of the rescue operation, something more than the ordinary had been happening—certainly something beyond the strictly human strategies planned and carried out by the rescue crews.

Contact had now been reestablished with the miners. This

had been accomplished by means of what was termed the *paloma mensajero*, literally translated "carrier pigeon," an ingenious system of transport that was the brainchild of Miguel Fortt, a well-known mining consultant who had given generously of his own time as a volunteer in the rescue. The *paloma,* as it was commonly referenced, was a three-meter (ten-foot) length of pipe only about seven centimeters (three inches) in diameter which could be threaded down through the narrow borehole from the surface to the miners' refuge. This permitted the rescue teams to send down food items, bottles of water, medicines, anything that would fit into the narrow space. It also permitted the miners to send up written messages and letters to their loved ones.

Among the first letters sent to the surface was one from Jorge Galleguillos, 56 years old, married, an underground miner all of his working life and certainly not a man known for wild imaginings. The letter was to his brother Eleodoro, also a career miner. The story it related was an astonishing one. Jorge Galleguillos and another miner, Franklin Lobos, a former soccer star, were the two men who had been driving from the workshop down toward the emergency shelter when the mine "sat," sending shock waves through the tunnels. As a rock slab collapsed behind them, both men swore they had witnessed just ahead a small white butterfly fluttering in the bright beam of their Nissan Terrano pickup's headlights.

White butterflies were not unknown in the desert. In spring months from September through November, when seasonal fogs rolling in from the Pacific Ocean added their own moisture to the usual nightly condensation, delicate purple flowers could be found blooming in scattered patches, their petals opening briefly in the early hours of dawn before the fierce desert sun arose. During this short blooming season, known as the "flowering desert," small white butterflies were a common enough sight, feeding from flower to flower while simultaneously pollinating the plants.

But in the full winter of August? And at this depth, more than half a kilometer beneath the surface? It was such an incredible sight that Franklin Lobos had instinctively hit the brakes, slowing the truck almost to a stop as the two men watched the butterfly flit across the tunnel. At that very instant, they were suddenly enveloped in an avalanche of dirt and pebbles. Far above them, the main rock collapse had already occurred, and now aftershocks were bringing down the tunnel walls and roof all around them.

"I couldn't see my hand in front of my face," Jorge Galleguillos wrote later to his brother. The rockfall was so extensive that it crushed a backhoe situated nearby. Not far ahead, a tank of water was completely buried in the rubble. Just ahead of the two men in the pickup, the tunnel was now littered with massive slabs of granite. If the vehicle had not slowed when it did, they too would have been crushed.

The tunnel behind Jorge Galleguillos and Franklin Lobos leading back to the surface was now completely blocked off. But once the dust settled, the two men were able to drive around and over the debris choking the tunnels ahead until they could join the other miners at the emergency shelter. Once they reached the others, they shared their experience with the white butterfly. The miracle of their narrow escape was one of the factors that helped the miners cling to hope as they waited for rescue.

Once Jorge's letter reached the surface, a new question began circulating. "What was the white butterfly? A real butterfly—or something else?"

Experts tried to give the story a scientific explanation. That one of these tiny, fragile butterflies would ever have flown of its own accord so far deep into the mine was virtually unthinkable. But perhaps the collapse of the mine itself had caused some anomalous downdraft within the ventilation system that carried fresh air from the surface to the deeper levels of the mine, sucking the creature down through a shaft from which it had emerged into the tunnel. This too seemed unlikely, considering that the nearest such patch of flowering desert was a full two kilometers away, and the season for both blooms and butterflies was a full month away. Could the miners have imagined the butterfly?

When asked, Jorge's brother Eleodoro, who had received the letter, responded simply, "I don't really know what that butterfly was. Maybe it was a little angel passing in front of them … saying, 'Hurry up, there's danger down here.'"

Miguel Fortt, the mining consultant who had devised the *paloma*, acknowledged the efforts to explain away the butterfly's appearance. "Maybe from a scientific perspective there is a physical possibility of a butterfly being carried by wind currents that far into the mine. You'll have to draw your own conclusions. But I can tell you that butterfly saved lives."

The two miners themselves who so narrowly missed being buried alive have no doubt that they were witnesses to a miracle, as they have both testified since. The warning they'd received from that small white butterfly had saved them from certain death.

Another question from the beginning had to do with the thirty-fourth person, listed when the roster of missing persons was handed out to the press as "NN, identity yet to be established." Who was this person? Another miner? It soon became clear that it was not. There were only thirty-three miners trapped below. Was it God? Because of all the astonishing happenings and unlikely nature of events that kept all thirty-three miners alive and made possible their ultimate rescue, those involved had no doubt of the answer.

Nelson Flores was one of the crew operating the drill that broke through to the refuge where the thirty-three miners had taken shelter. He shared his own recollection of that moment: "We were drilling downward through a shaft, the drill bit constantly spitting up dirt as it bored through solid rock. Suddenly there was no more dirt, just air beneath the drill bit. I was overjoyed, emotional. I let the boss know, and he went to inform the others."

Nelson continued, "We immediately stopped drilling to see if there was someone down there. We began to hear noises coming up through the metal of the drill probe. We put a stethoscope to the drill, and we could feel vibrations that could be someone hammering on the far end of the drill. But we still weren't completely convinced. So we took a hammer and struck the drill ourselves. Immediately we felt more hammering from below coming through the metal of the drill. That was when all the authorities in charge of the rescue operation arrived."

When his shift finished at the end of the day, I had the opportunity to talk with Nelson Flores. The emotion of having found the miners alive was still audible in his voice as he told me, "This was a fifty-fifty operation."

"What do you mean fifty-fifty?" I asked him.

"We as the operators did the best we could for our part. But the other half came from"—he made a gesture upward—"you know Who up there, because that probe went off course toward the refuge."

It was common for such boreholes to drift off course by at least 5 percent during the drilling process. Over a distance of 700 meters, this translated to 35–40 meters (110–130 feet), one reason the probes had proved so unreliable in locating the miners' refuge. Despite all efforts, this particular probe had gone off course during the last segment of the drilling. The direction and drift of the deviation had proved exactly far enough to pierce through at the very corner where tunnel wall met roof a few meters from the emergency shelter. If this hadn't happened, the probe would have continued its trajectory exactly without ever making contact like its fellow probe three days earlier. Because of the manner in which the probe had deviated off course just enough to break through to the miners, that particular drill came to be christened with a very special nickname: "the Hand of God."

Certainly the miners as well as their families were convinced. It was a letter from Jimmy Sánchez, the youngest of the trapped miners and a Copiapó native, writing from more than 700 meters below the earth, that in the last paragraph declared unequivocally, "We were 34 because God never abandoned us!"

Jimmy Sánchez wasn't referring to some literal appearance of God in the form of a man or by means of an angel. But the miners experienced His presence every moment of their captivity—constant, protective, caring. And so, in every sense, very real!

8

LIGHT IN THE DARKNESS

Festivities celebrating the discovery of all thirty-three miners alive and well spread across the entire country as the Chilean people came together in an explosion of joy and relief, even those bitterly divided by political, social, or labor issues. There would be plenty of time in the future for recriminations and complaint. But for today at least, these were laid aside.

I lived the celebration up at the mine along with the rest of the residents of Camp Hope. With the growing number of journalists and rescue crews, this was now a large crowd of at least 2000 people.

President Piñera climbed to the knoll of the hill where the commemorative flags waved in the wind. From there he once again read the paper he'd read when he'd first descended from the presidential helicopter. We eventually learned that the note had been taped to the end of the probe by 47-year-old José Ojeda, a widower with twenty-seven years' experience as a miner.

"This is truly a miracle," the president added, waving the paper in its sealed plastic bag.

None of us were unmoved, an effervescence of joy bubbling up in each of us so that we could not keep still. We jumped up and down, embraced, laughed, cried. The news crews were running around from one side to the other, trying to keep up with the president. As they dragged their equipment cables behind them, these writhed and tripped and tangled as though they too were living creatures dancing and celebrating.

Still, in our euphoria, no one lost sight of the true reality of this moment. This was a miracle, as the president himself had reminded us all. Across Chile and around the world, the celebrating multitudes acknowledged this miracle and gave praise to God.

For some reason—I can't remember now what prompted it; God knows—I made up my mind during the celebration to give a Bible to President Sebastian Piñera and Minister of Mines Laurence Golborne just like the Bibles I had distributed to the trapped miners' families. I took two I still had, wrote a dedication inside, then went to look for the two men. I was stopped at a police barricade set up between the camp and the mine entrance. The guards wouldn't let me go forward.

Assuming the president and minister would eventually have to pass by this direction, I lingered near the barricade, waiting for them. But a short time later, I spotted the presidential helicopter lifting off the ground and heading across the desert in the direction of Santiago, the nation's capital. While I was feeling somewhat frustrated, there was nothing I could do about it.

There will be another opportunity sometime, I consoled myself.

I returned to the celebration. Several regional supermarkets had donated quantities of food and drinks which had been set out in the communal dining tent. The tent swarmed with a large crowd eating and drinking. Near the entrance to the tent, I ran into a well-known Chilean television reporter, Amaro Gómez-Pablo, along with Senator Isabel Allende. We hugged each other, expressing our joy over the day's events. Then Amaro spoke up.

"Pastor, Senator, shall we offer a toast to the miners?"

In order to prevent problems in this emotional, high-stress environment, alcoholic beverages were not served at the camp, though there were those who brought in their own. But darkness had now fallen, the hour for hot chocolate, which was offered every evening as a palliative against the chill of the desert night. The three of us were each holding a cup of hot chocolate. So Amaro added jokingly, "Yes, let's toast, even if only with hot chocolate."

We raised a joyful toast to the miners and then separated. But the evening was not yet over. A short time later, on the huge television screen that broadcast news coverage to the camp, I saw two familiar figures: Amaro Gómez-Pablo and Minister of Mines Laurence Golborne. The television reporter was interviewing Minister Golborne.

"Where could they be?" I asked myself. I looked around me on all sides. Then I spotted the pair standing near the police barrier set up not far from me between the entrance to the dining tent and the mouth of the mine a short distance down the road. Only a few people gathered around the pair. I lingered near the barrier as I waited for Amaro Gómez-Pablo to finish his interview with the minister.

Meanwhile, I prayed silently, "Lord, if it be Your will, please let the minister remain behind alone when the interview is finished so that I can talk with him."

And that is exactly what happened. As the interview finished, the participants headed back toward the very spot where I was standing near the barrier. Of course there weren't a lot of alternatives, since the entire camp area was relatively small and open. As Minister Golborne approached me, I spoke up. "Minister, I have a gift here for you."

Stopping, the minister smiled at me and nodded. "Yes, I see, tell me about it."

"Well, what I have here with me is a Bible identical to the ones we gave out last Thursday to each of the families of the thirty-three trapped miners."

"That's wonderful!" he exclaimed. "I applaud you for such a kind act."

"And this one here is for you. Please accept it with our deep appreciation. The inscription written inside says that this is in recognition of your dedication and commitment to help in any way possible in finding and rescuing the miners."

The surroundings in which we stood were unpretentious ones for an encounter with such a distinguished VIP but appropriate to this occasion. All around us were the works of God's own hand. The black, rounded silhouettes against a starry sky that were the hills in whose bowels lay buried Chile's immense mineral wealth. The nocturnal mist locals call *camanchaca*, which had rolled in from the Pacific Ocean with the evening chill, pooling as a heavy white fog in the gullies between hills, swirling as feathery wisps among the tents and mobile trailers. The campfires without which the chill of night would be unbearable, flickering their cheerful red and orange flames in front of each tent. The noisy crowd celebrating today's miracle inside and all around the dining tent. And of course, invisible to us but ever-present in our thoughts, the miners celebrating this miracle as well down in the depths of the mine.

"Thank you very much for this," Minister Golborne said to me, emotion tingeing his voice. Then he gave me a hug as though he felt, as I did, the grandeur of this incredible day.

This was the perfect moment. I couldn't let it pass.

"Minister," I told him, "there is something weighing on my heart. I would like to send thirty-three Bibles down into the mine, one for each of the miners."

In my mind was the thought that a Bible would be one way I could help the miners in the prolonged wait facing them, already protracted beyond the limits of normal human patience, especially considering the situation of extreme crisis in which they continued to find themselves. The comfort of God's Word and His promises available in Scripture could help the miners bear up under the various physical, emotional, or spiritual difficulties that were bound to appear—if the miners had access to them.

"How could you possibly do this," Minister Golborne asked me, "considering that the *paloma* only has a diameter of 7.5 centimeters?" This is a width of only about three inches.

Without being sure myself a Bible that small even existed, I responded, "Minister, just give me the authorization to find a Bible that size."

"Well," he answered, "if you find one, you can bring it to me."

I immediately began the search. I called up my district supervisor, Pastor Francisco Briseño. He got in contact with Casa Editora

Sudamericana, the Adventist publishing house in Santiago. They didn't have a Bible that small, but the president commissioned their administrative director, Derik Orellana, to try to find one. He contacted the International Bible Society. As soon as business opened on Monday, August 23, my helpers began calling as well any Christian bookstore or distributor that sold Bibles. Soon I received a call that a Bible had been found, but it was 12 centimeters across. That was too big. We continued the search. Another was found just 9 centimeters. Still too big.

"Please keep searching," I asked.

"We've checked with every place that sells Bibles," I was told.

"Just keep looking, please. There has to be one no more than 7.5 centimeters."

When I received a final phone call that afternoon, I sent up heartfelt thanks to God. The voice on the phone informed me excitedly, "Carlos, I have found a Bible that is only 7 centimeters across."

It was the Bible we were looking for. I answered promptly, "Please, buy the Bibles and send them as quickly as you can. By special air freight, whatever it takes, but send them without delay. I need them now already."

That same Monday afternoon, a meeting was scheduled in the big dining tent of Camp Hope between the mayors of the four municipalities closest to San José Mine and the family members of the trapped miners. The purpose for the meeting was to offer legal representation to the families as well as the miners themselves in relationship to the owners of the mine. By now, additional shortfalls in mine safety had come to light. Among them were the ventilation shafts that led down into the mine. Several feet across, these not only permitted fresh air to circulate inside the mine but were intended to offer an escape route in case of just such a disaster as had occurred. According to safety regulations, ladders should have extended the length of the ventilation shafts. But the mine owners had not bothered to have them installed, and with the additional avalanches after the original mine collapse, the ventilation shafts were now sealed shut in any case.

But once the trapped miners had been able to share their own experiences, it came to light that they had made an effort to climb out that way. If the ladders had been in place, they would have had ample time to reach the surface before the additional rock-falls cut off escape. Furious, the families were demanding that the mine owners be held accountable and forced to make compensation. To compound the injustice, the mine owners had not been paying the salaries of the trapped miners since the accident.

The four mayors present were Brunilda González, mayor of Caldera, in whose jurisdiction the San José Mine actually fell; then in order of geographic proximity, Maglio Cicardini, mayor of Copiapó, who was able to participate only by teleconference; Carlos Barahona, mayor of Tierra Amarilla; and Cristian Tapia, mayor of Ballenar, who was the most frequent visitor to the mine during the seventy days of the rescue operation.

While the other mayors were chatting with different family groups, I approached Brunilda González, whom I had met on other occasions. "Mayor, I am Pastor Carlos Parra."

"Yes, I have seen you working around the camp," she answered graciously.

"If it's possible, I'd like to speak with the family members."

"Yes, of course; as soon as the mayors are finished, it will be your turn."

The dining tent was filled with relatives of the trapped miners. All were attentive, most interested in what the mayors had to say. The four explained what the families needed to do to secure their legal rights related to back wages and current salaries for the miners as well as other legal avenues they could pursue to force the mine owners to pay compensation to the miners.

When they were all finished, Mayor González announced, "And now we'd like to give a few minutes to Pastor Carlos Parra, whom you have all seen working here in the camp since the beginning of this emergency. He has something he'd like to share with you all."

I began to speak. "What is on my heart is that I would like to send a Bible to each of your loved ones who is down in the mine. I've already spoken about this with the minister of mines. But since you are the ones who decide what happens with your loved ones, I wanted to ask if you would approve such an initiative."

The group broke into spontaneous applause. I went on, "Minister Golborne has asked me how I can possibly carry out such a project when the space available in the delivery tube, the *paloma*, is only 7.5 centimeters wide."

Then I shared with them the search we'd made for a Bible that would be small enough, along with the good news that we'd found one only 7 centimeters across.

"Tomorrow they will arrive here in the camp," I finished. The family members welcomed the news with more applause and cheers. Their applause was all the approval I needed to go forward with the project.

The next day while we waited for the Bibles to arrive, I occupied myself with another very special event. With the news that all thirty-three miners had been discovered alive, the Gypsy congregation from Copiapó was determined to offer up their thanksgiving to God for answered prayer at the site where the miracle had transpired. So they organized a sizable group to travel again to Camp Hope. The Romany people's traditional festivals always include a lot of food and lively music. Since these Gypsies were a Christian group, their music was just as lively but full of praises to God and joyous expressions of their own personal faith.

The Gypsies arrived with a large tent of their own, which they quickly raised. With their traditional colorful costumes and instruments, they immediately drew everyone's attention. They invited the entire camp to share the meal they were preparing. Already prepared ahead of time, this was a simple, but delicious feast. There were *niños envueltos* (literally, "wrapped infants"), a dish served traditionally at Gypsy festivals, which consisted of highly seasoned rice, meat, boiled eggs, vegetables, and tomato sauce, all rolled into cabbage leaves and steamed or baked. Accompanying the cabbage rolls was a traditional Chilean salad along with fruit juices and other nonalcoholic drinks.

As the food was set out, the group sang and played their instruments. Their soloist, Yanko, a Copiapó native, is well known in this region for his outstanding singing talent and traditional flamenco dancing. He reminded the crowd of the purpose for the group's prior visit to the camp: to pray onsite that God would watch over the miners and guide the rescue crews to find them.

"Now we have come to offer thanks to God for answering all

our prayers, since He has indeed protected the miners, keeping them both alive and well. All thirty-three are well, thanks to God."

Family members and journalists alike crowded around to enjoy the feast. The Gypsy group's lively Romany music was a breath of fresh air blowing through the camp, at times so joyous and playful that it set feet to tapping, other times sweet, melancholic, nostalgic. But the nostalgia in those haunting melodies held no sadness but rather the spiritual nostalgia of a soul that has found in Christ its complete satisfaction and so can never again feel truly whole apart from Christ.

One Red Cross volunteer was so deeply touched by the Gypsy group's music and sharing that she gave her life to Christ right there on the spot. The Gypsies distributed thirty-three CDs containing the music they had sung, one for each of the trapped miners' families. Since the announcement that the trapped miners had been found alive, the media presence at San José Mine had been greatly augmented by international news crews. The neat lines of their campers and trailers now filled one side of the camp, in stark contrast to the modest shelters of the miner families, swelling the population of the camp to over 2000. As a result, the next day on the news, many media outlets reported on the Gypsy congregation's visit to Camp Hope.

Meanwhile the miniature Bibles had finally arrived. My family helped me prepare them for their descent into the mine. Gloria, my wife, took out the list of the thirty-three miners and began copying their names one at a time into the Bibles. To each she added the text of Isaiah 41:10: "Do not fear, for I am with you; do not be dismayed, for I am your God."

We also attached a sticker that gave our church contact information as the donors of the Bibles and my own phone number as pastor, along with the inscription: "We are praying for your rescue."

My thirteen-year-old son, Malachi, and ten-year-old daughter, Belén, marked in bright colors specific Bible texts that would offer to the miners a message of hope and comfort in God. Among them were the following:

"Have I not commanded you? Be strong and courageous. Do not be afraid; do not be discouraged, for the Lord your God will be with you wherever you go" (Joshua 1:9).

"I waited patiently for the Lord; he turned to me and heard my cry. He lifted me out of the slimy pit, out of the mud and mire. He set my feet on a rock and gave me a firm place to stand. He put a new song in my mouth, a hymn of praise to our God" (Psalm 40:1–3).

This final text became the point of strongest spiritual support for the miners and their family members, especially the phrase: "He lifted me out of the slimy pit," or as the words ran in the Spanish: "the pit of desperation." For the trapped miners in their time of desperation, that promise offered a rock-solid foundation of faith and hope.

Once the Bibles were ready, I prepared to take the Bibles up to Minister of Mines Laurence Golborne so that he could deliver them to the miners. But that morning, Wednesday, August 25, I heard on the news that he had returned to Santiago. Since he was the one who had approved the project, this seemed an insurmountable difficulty. But God had orchestrated all this for good up to this point. I had to trust that He would not stop doing so now.

The same news brief announced that Minister of Health Jaime

Mañalich would be taking over Minister Golborne's position of leadership at Camp Hope. Taking the Bibles, I drove up to San José Mine to talk to the minister. When I found him, I said, "Minister Mañalich, I have already spoken with Minister Golborne, and he was in agreement with me to send a Bible to each miner. Now that you are in charge of operations, I'd like to know if we can still send them."

"Sure, no problem," the minister responded immediately. "I have only one restriction. This needs to be a private donation, not public. We can't call together the media every time someone wants to send something to the miners. If you want to involve the press in this, it will have to be your own affair in which we will not officially participate."

Since the purpose for all of this was to help the miners, nothing else, his restriction was certainly not a problem for me. While we waited for the final go-ahead to send the Bibles down, another church member and I set up a table near the camp entrance. We piled the Bibles on them and hung up a sign that read, "Let us continue praying for the miners."

A journalist was walking past as we did so, hardly a surprise since the camp covered only a small area and by now was crowded with hundreds of news crews. The journalist approached me to ask, "Excuse me. Are you going to be selling those Bibles?"

"No," I answered. "We are getting ready to send these Bibles down to the miners through the *paloma*."

"Really? Do you mind if I write up a press release on this?"

"Not at all, go right ahead."

He had barely asked his interview questions before the entire press corps, national and international, hurried over to do the same. They crowded around, clamoring for personal interviews. One of them asked, "Do the authorities know about this?"

"Yes, of course," I responded. "The minister of mines already approved it. In fact, these Bibles are already dedicated, each one with the name of the miner to whom it is being sent."

A little while later in private, I was able to hand over the Bibles to Minister Mañalich.

"One is for you," I told him, giving him a copy. He immediately began to leaf through its pages.

"As you can see, certain texts are marked in color," I added.

He found the marked psalm and began to read: "I waited patiently for the Lord; he turned to me and heard my cry. He lifted me out of the slimy pit, out of the mud and mire."

Visibly moved, he said to me, "Wow, it's as if God Himself wrote these words specifically to the miners."

I expressed my agreement and then requested from him an interview for Radio Nuevo Tiempo. He agreed readily. In the interview, he read aloud the same psalm for the comfort of all the listeners to the program.

The sending of the Bibles to the miners proved an appealing human interest story to the international press. I found myself being interviewed by journalists from five different continents. These included news crews from as far afield as Al-Jazeera, based in the Middle East, and as nearby as neighboring Argentina and Brazil. The journalist from the Brazilian media network Globo ("World") aired the most complete interview, a twenty-five-minute program that was broadcast across Brazil.

At the conclusion of the interview, he asked, "What can one possibly send to these miners by means of the *paloma*, a probe of only 7.5 centimeters in diameter? How can one possibly package hope and send it down to the miners? Well, Pastor Carlos Parra has managed to do just that with these miniature Bibles, inside which comforting texts have been highlighted in bright colors to bring hope to the miners."

On Thursday, August 26, exactly three weeks after the mine collapse, as soon as the essential food and medicines had been delivered to the miners, the Bibles were sent down. In order to produce a Bible so diminutive, the print was of necessity also tiny, the pages very thin. So each Bible was accompanied by a small magnifying glass to make reading more comfortable. These were the first nonessential articles to be sent down into the mine.

Or rather, the Bibles were very much an essential provision for the emotional and spiritual well-being of the miners. Now each miner had a Bible to meet his personal spiritual needs during the long wait that would be ahead of them.

9

MORE DISCOURAGEMENT

That same Thursday, the coordinators for the rescue operation determined that they should prepare three separate plans of action—Plan A, B, and C.

Plan A would use one of the world's largest drilling rigs, the Strata 950, which was capable of drilling a shaft almost a meter wide to a depth of several kilometers. The drawback was its speed. This plan would take four months to accomplish, leaving the miners trapped below until Christmas.

Plan B would use a more powerful American-made drill, the Schramm T-130. This drill could reach the miners in a much shorter time, but it was not designed for precision drilling at such depths. Just like the earlier probes, it could easily drift off course at deeper levels, missing the miners altogether.

Plan C was to use a massive petroleum rig that took an entire convoy to transport its towers, generators, tubing, and machinery up to the mine. Its platform alone was as long as a soccer field. This equipment was even more powerful and capable of precision drilling, but simply getting it into operation would take at least a month.

The decision was made to go forward with all three plans simultaneously, so that if one broke down or failed, no time would be lost in going forward with another. The existence of three plans, with the huge investment of equipment, personnel, and cost this entailed, was an indicator of the Chilean government's commitment and absolute determination to do everything within their power to rescue the miners.

For all three plans, the rescue would take between three and four months. If four months, it would not happen until Christmas. So now the rescue operation faced a new challenge. Their earlier objective had been simply to find the miners and establish contact with them. This now accomplished, their new objective was to retrieve them safely from the mine by Christmas Day. This would be a massive enterprise involving many different tasks. Some of these were related to the health and well-being of the trapped miners, others to the drilling of a shaft through which they could escape, and still others to taking care of the families. Altogether, even though family members and rescue crews were now assured that the miners were alive and well, keeping them that way and getting them out alive would be an extremely complicated and difficult undertaking.

To begin with, in the joy of discovering all thirty-three men alive and well, neither the families nor the general public had taken much notice of statements that the rescue could take until

My first contact with Camp Hope was as one of fifteen pastors from the Association of Evangelical Pastors of Copiapó who went as a group to pray for the miners and their families. From the top of this rocky hilltop – which soon became the symbolic focal point for the hopes of everyone at Camp Hope – we earnestly sought God's blessing and guidance for the rescue operation.

Along the summit of the hill were planted a semicircle of Chilean flags, one for each of the trapped miners. Over the next weeks, most press conferences and official announcements were given here.

Family members braved the elements to set up camp near the entrance of the mine. With the addition of rescue personnel, media crews, and volunteer workers, the encampment continued to grow until there were eventually more than 2000 people living there.

Families gathered around fires not only to warm themselves against the chill of the Atacama Desert, but to unite in support of each other. These brave people gave up the comforts of home and the security of jobs to show solidarity with their loved ones, not knowing what the final outcome would be.

My first impulse to serve the community at Camp Hope centred on the children who, I felt, needed immediate attention. What better distraction to cheer up children than by interacting with other youth like themselves? These enthusiastic Pathfinders not only brought happiness to the children, but in so doing uplifted the parents' spirits as well.

With María Segovia, Camp Hope's 'mayor'. It was a pleasure to witness the growing leadership of this woman, always so dynamic and hardworking but demonstrating as well a deep spiritual sensitivity and closeness to God.

With nothing much to occupy their time during the day, the families needed to concentrate their thoughts on something healthier than their anxiety and despair. I felt inspired to provide each family with a Bible and had soon set up an improvised 'office' from which to hand out these hope-inspiring books.

Presenting a Bible to family members of miner Osman Araya.

The Gypsy congregation that was under my pastoral supervision giving thanks to God for the miracle that all the miners had been discovered alive. These Gypsy Christians express their faith in God through music that is lively and full of joyous expressions of their own personal faith.

With Ramon Curin, one of my congregation's leaders and a paramedic who was of great support in prayer and work during my ministry at Camp Hope.

Working together with my church, we were able to source Bibles that would be small enough to send down to the miners by way of the *paloma*. Here I am presenting these miniature Bibles to Minister of Health Jaime Mañalich.

One of the miniature Bibles,
measuring only 7 cm across.

The whole evangelical community was supporting the miners and their families during this time. At
the bicentennial celebrations were Bishop Eduardo Durán, senior pastor of the Evangelical Cathedral
of Santiago (centre), and Reverand Alfredo Cooper, Protestant chaplain to the president's palace (right).

I was privileged to be able to invite the chamber choir from the Adventist University in Chillán to inspire hope through their gospel music at the bicentennial celebrations. They chose majestic, spiritual songs that expressed deep faith, hope, and praise to God. Here they pose with Director Susana Orvalle (green jacket) and the Regional Governor of Atacama (center).

On behalf of the families, I was privileged to present a Bible to President Piñera, both in celebration of the bicentennial and in recognition of all that he had done for the miners and his role in the miracle God had accomplished.

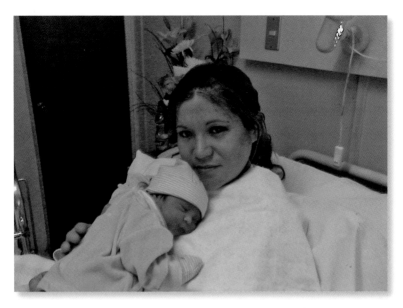

Baby Esperanza – originally intended to be named Carolina – was born on September 14, 2010 while her father, Ariel Ticona, was still trapped in the mine. Ariel and his wife, Elizabeth Segovia, chose instead the name 'Esperanza' because of the hope of new life that she represented.

With Rolly the Clown, whose gentle, comical humor and mischievous pranks during the bicentennial celebrations endeared him to Camp Hope children and adults alike. When the children begged him to stay on, an agreement was reached with his employers and Rolly became the official "clown of Camp Hope."

On Saturday, October 9, the Schramm T-130 drill broke through to where the thirty-three miners had been trapped since August 5. They had now endured two months and four days without seeing a ray of sunlight. The cheers that had been raised so many times during the last two months once again rang out: "Chi-chi-chi! Le-le-le! Viva Chile! Long live the miners of Chile!"

The last prayer vigil with the family members lasted from midnight on October 12 – when the rescue began – to midnight October 13 when the last miner emerged. Our objective was very specific: to pray that the rescue operation would be completed without incident and with every miner safely free.

The letter from Jimmy Sánchez, the youngest of the miners, in which he expresses his conviction that God was the thirty-fourth miner among them.

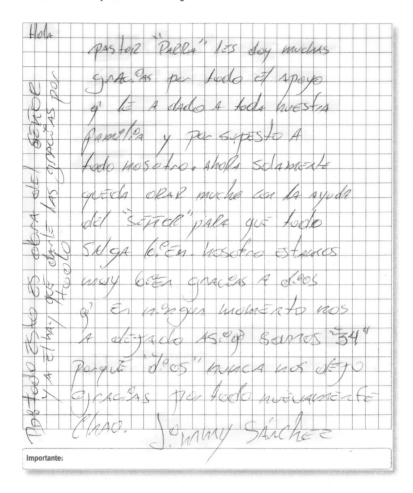

Hello

Pastor Parra, I thank you very much for all the support you have given to our family and of course, to all of us. Now it only remains to pray a lot that with the Lord's help everything goes well. We are very well, thanks to God who has never abandoned us. There are actually "34" of us because God has never left us down here.

Thanks again for everything brother.

Jimmy Sanchez

P.S. This is the work of the Lord and we must thank Him for everything.

Pastor: Carlos PARRA DiAz

De aqui abajo le saludo a
Ud. y familia por sus oraciones
para nosotros los 33 mineros. te
Contare que aqui estamos todos tranquilo
y se que Dios el todo poderoso nos A
protegido del primer dia que paso esto
le contare que aqui se ora A Los
12:00 P.M todos Los Dias de ocurrido esto.
Aqui hay de todo Credo, Religion.
todos Hermanos en dios. Me cuesta un
poco Escribir... se siente algo DENtro que
Me es Dificil pensar... Si Dios nos
A DEjado con ViDP Es porque algo nos
Tiene preparado para cuando salgamos.
Aqui Ahi mucho Tiempo para pensar y
oror. Para Ud y familia:

"Sólo Jesús nos
Hace descansar, de Tal manera que nuestro
pesoda carga se convierte en algo Liviano y
fácil de llevar. De esta manera se nos
ABre un panorama lleno de esperanza,
Donde las Aflixiones se Tornan en un
Tuturo Consolador!!

Se despide de Ud y toda
Su familia

José Ricardo Ojeda V.
"Corazón DE Minero"

The letter from José Ojeda, the 'poet' among the miners, who found inspiration in this time of crisis.
I was deeply touched by the profound spirituality of this hardworking, blue-collar laborer, his deep
faith and close relationship with God shining through every word of his simple phrases.

[Jose Ojeda's letter]:

To Pastor Carlos Parra Díaz

From down here I greet you and your family. Thanks for your prayers for us the 33 miners. I can tell you that here we are all calm and I know that God the Almighty has protected us from the first day this happened.

Here we pray at 12:00 noon every day since the day that this happened.

Here there are of every creed and religion, all brothers in God. I have some difficulties writing ... I feel something inside that makes it difficult to think ... If God has left us alive it is because He has prepared something for us when we get out. Down here we have plenty of time to think and pray.

For you and your family, "Only Jesus makes us rest, in a way that our burdens become light and easy to carry. In this way it opens a view full of hope, where the troubles are transformed into a comforting future."

Goodbye to you and your family

José Ricardo Ojeda
"Heart Of a Miner"

Being interviewed by TV journalist and news anchor Amaro Gómez-Pablos for TVN (Televisión Nacional de Chile).

Omar Reygadas, 56, kneels down with his miniature Bible in hand, giving testimony to the faith that had sustained him during his long days of captivity. I was pleasantly surprised to see that many of the miners were clutching this symbol of hope as they emerged from their entrapment.

After stepping out of the Phoenix capsule, thirty-one year old Alex Vega drew attention to the message on his t-shirt, "¡Gracias, Señor!" ("Thank You, Lord!") On the back of the t-shirt are printed words from Psalm 95:4, "In His hand are the depths of the earth, and the mountain peaks belong to Him." Many of the miners chose to wear these T-shirts – a gift from the Chilean branch of Campus Crusade – during their ride to the surface as a declaration of their gratitude to God for the miracle of their rescue.

After the rescue at the hospital with miner Raul Bustos, who said, "I will never leave this little Bible."

I was delighted to spend some time with the miners at the Copiapó Hospital after the rescue. As I visited with each miner, the quickest way to establish a connection was in reference to the miniature Bible that had been sent down to them. The moment I introduced myself as Pastor Parra who had sent the Bibles, an immediate bond was established, their appreciation and pleasure manifest as we spoke.

My family who supported me during my ministry at Camp Hope: son Carlos Malaquías (Malachi), daughter Belén, and my wife, Gloria.

Christmas. On the contrary, the focus was on the bicentennial of Chile's independence, just three weeks away. Somehow an idea had spread that it would be possible to dig 700 meters into solid rock to release the miners in time for the bicentennial festivities.

While celebrating continued, it didn't take long for the reality to sink in that a long wait lay ahead. Minister of Mines Laurence Golborne made a public disavowal of the optimistic rumors that the miners would be aboveground by the bicentennial celebration scheduled for September 18. In a press conference, he stated firmly that the best-case prognosis was a wait of three to four months.

"I've been hearing crazy rumors such as that we are going to get the miners out by the Bicentennial. I would be delighted if those rumors were true. Perhaps if we had access to a better technology, such as Superman with his laser rays, we could do so. But to this point we haven't come up with anything that would permit us to carry out an operation like this in such a short time."

Fresh discouragement seized hold of everyone. For both the miners and their family members, emotions seesawed from one extreme to the other. On the one side, everyone felt happiness that the miners were alive. On the other side was anguish because they were still trapped. And then the uncertainty: could the rescue crews really get them out?

Perhaps the most logical thing to do now that the miners had been found alive would have been to send everyone home to return to their daily lives without the constant stress and anxiety of watching the rescue operation every moment, day after day. There would be plenty of time in the future, when the actual moment of rescue arrived, to fret over its dangers and problems.

Meanwhile four months lay ahead that were made even longer by their uncertainty.

But the families were determined to stay at the mine until they saw their loved ones brought out alive. So Camp Hope not only remained but continued to grow as more rescue crews, more journalists, more experts and medical personnel and mechanics poured in. Once again the question came to me: What could I do to help these people during this long wait? It was one thing to help the trapped miners down in the mine, cut off from their regular daily routines, with endless time now to meditate on spiritual things—or to slip gradually into madness, if they focused only on their imprisonment. Sending down the Bibles was all I could do for them. But what about their families?

One thing I could do. And that was to pray. To continue praying. Not as before, pleading for the miracle of life for the miners. But now with a new request, that God would accelerate the time of their rescue. That God would cut short the waiting time despite the limitations imposed by our current available technology. That He would hasten the progress of the machines, increase their efficiency, remove any obstacles and accidents. God had already given the miracle of life. The miners had all survived. Now we needed a new miracle, the miracle of a new technology not available to the rescue crews.

"Father, give us what we with our technology don't have," I prayed. "Give us the gift of time."

We also needed to pray in a different fashion, a new way. How? I had no great answers myself. But as God had answered so many other prayers, He placed an idea in my mind that would not go away: a worldwide prayer chain. Of course! What better way to bring together all the people around the world who had been following this story and praying for the miners, so that we could raise a united plea to God for what would be needed in this rescue?

A worldwide prayer chain, that's it, I said to myself. *Thank You, Lord, You have shown me what we need to do, and we will do it.*

Two days later, María Segovia, the popularly acclaimed "mayor" of Camp Hope, offered me a commentary based on her own observations. The deep sense of spirituality that had been so evident in the camp all these weeks had diminished since the miners had been found alive. It should have been the other way around. God had done exactly what we had so often pleaded for in preserving the lives of all the miners. So how could we not all be overflowing with gratitude to God for His answered prayer?

But as is so typical with human beings, the initial flood of joy and gratitude had soon ebbed under the dreary routine of one dismal, uncertain day after another. María understood the phenomenon. Both the miners and their families would now have to wait three to four more months before seeing their loved ones. The prospect of such a long wait was gradually swallowing up the sense of gratitude they had all experienced that first day—especially since no one could be sure the long wait would result in a successful rescue.

As María commented on this to me, she went on, "Pastor, we should continue having prayer times with the entire group, because since we found out the miners are alive, I have seen our spirit of prayer and unity here in the camp beginning to fade away."

I brought up the idea for a worldwide prayer chain. She enthusiastically endorsed the plan. The next question was what would be the best time of day for a collective prayer session? One possibility was 12 noon. Since their first days imprisoned underground, even before they'd been discovered alive, the trapped miners had been meeting together for prayer every day at noon under the direction of 56-year-old José Henríquez, a godly Christian man and active lay leader in his church, who had become the spiritual leader of the group. In fact, José had been sharing with the miners customized Bible studies, created by Baptist pastor Marcelo Leiva, to help them through their ordeal. Also assisting José Henríquez in giving spiritual leadership to the trapped miners was Omar Reygadas, a widowed career miner, 56, who was undergoing at this moment his third serious disaster of the dangerous profession he'd chosen. There was also Osmar Araya, a miner only by default, since he'd been a fruit picker until this job. Before the mine collapse Osmar had publicly expressed his own concerns over the unsafe working conditions. All three miners were devout Christians.

While praying at the same time as the trapped miners would have been a pleasurable choice, a second option that seemed more convenient for the families was in the early evening at 6 p.m. The families already came together each day at that hour to meet with rescue operation and government authorities. This was the hour when announcements and the latest reports concerning the miners were given. No one missed these meetings. Since the families had already formed the daily habit of gathering at that hour in the dining tent, it seemed a more logical choice. Even better, at that hour the rescue operation and government personnel could participate as well.

I spoke with Angélica Álvarez, who had earlier told me, "God has a purpose in all this." By now her influence as a leader in the camp was far-reaching.

"I'd like to start a worldwide prayer chain to ask God that the rescue happen long before Christmas, when the officials say they hope to reach the men," I told her.

"Of course, Pastor, that would be a wonderful idea," she responded.

"And I was thinking that the best time and place would be right here in the dining tent at 6 p.m. when you are already here as families meeting with the government authorities. Would that be a possibility?" She concurred that this would be the best hour.

I went next to talk with Christian Jahn, who, as the regional secretary in charge of the Department of Planning and Coordination (SERPLAC) for the Copiapó region, was currently the top government official here at the camp.

"No, you can't enter the assembly place for the daily government briefing," he informed me bluntly. "It isn't allowed. Only government officials and the actual members of the miners' families are allowed access."

I returned to let Angélica Álvarez know what had happened. She said to me, "Pastor, leave this issue with me. I'll see what we can do."

She went to speak with the regional secretary. She informed him that I was a pastor, the chaplain of Camp Hope, who had been with the families since the very beginning and had been of great help and support to the hurting family members. "We want him to be with us every day at 6 p.m. so that before you give your own reports, we can pray together and read the Bible."

Since the protests that had followed President Piñera's first visit to Camp Hope, the Chilean government had been careful to respect the desires of the miners' families. At a practical level, it was their decisions that determined all the activities of the camp.

"If this is what you want," he answered, "I have no problem with it."

Coming to speak to me, Secretary Jahn let me know, "Pastor, you are welcome to enter the assembly any time you want to."

From that day forward, the regional government gave me official credentials that identified me as pastor and chaplain of Camp Hope. For the next forty days, the evening government briefing began always with a time of Bible reading, a brief devotional, and prayer, lasting altogether about ten minutes. Everyone took part without any distinction of denomination or church creed. At that moment there was only one spiritual creed: we were all Christians together worshipping the same God. We all believed in God, we lifted our praise to Him, we prayed to Him as one, and He was our answer to every need.

El Mercurio, the Santiago daily newspaper, published the following concerning this nightly activity: "Pastor Carlos Parra has been one of the religious representatives most visible in the camp. He is there virtually every day, visiting with the families and organizing activities of worship and praise with cheerful, enthusiastic music. He has also organized a worldwide prayer chain that takes place every day at 6 p.m., to pray that the rescue will be made possible well in advance of the four months originally announced. Just a couple of weeks ago, Minister of Mines Golborne approached this pastor to tell him, 'God is listening to your prayers; keep praying!'"

To extend this prayer chain worldwide, we used every means of communication available to us at the camp—the Internet, e-mail, a Facebook page, Christian radio, and the communication network of our own denomination. From around the world, we heard of countless others who were praying with us for the miners' quick release.

The miners' own family members were now sending letters down to their loved ones that told of the prayers being offered for them. When they found out about the worldwide prayer chain at 6 p.m. every evening, they began to pray together at that hour along with their usual noon prayer time. Two of the miners wrote me personal letters regarding this. One was José Ricardo Ojeda.

His letter read, "From here below I send greetings to you and your family in appreciation of your prayers for us, the 33 miners. I can tell you that down here we are all fine and tranquil, and I have absolute assurance that God Almighty has been protecting us since the very first day when all this happened."

That letter would later be read in its entirety in a more public forum than I had ever imagined. We were now praying as a group at Camp Hope every single evening. But we postponed the official launch of the worldwide prayer chain for the afternoon of September 2. This was because I'd had an invitation to travel to Brasilia, the capital of Brazil, for a few days prior to that date to speak at a conference of our denominational leaders on what was happening at the San José Mine. I took advantage of that trip to share our plans for the worldwide prayer chain, so that they too could promote this united prayer front within their own congregations and ministry zones. Meanwhile Radio Nuevo Tiempo was already announcing that on Thursday, September 2, we would be officially launching the worldwide prayer chain from Camp Hope.

By now, thanks to the ingenuity of Pedro Gallo, a phone line had been run through the borehole, permitting those on the surface to speak to loved ones trapped in the mine. They now shared in detail the horrors of those first seventeen days when no one had known if they were still alive. Miraculously, all thirty-three men had made it to the emergency shelter without serious injuries. Once the mountain had stopped shaking, and the dust and dirt had settled, they'd been able to take stock of their situation. Exploration soon revealed that the tunnels were hopelessly blocked. Attempts to climb out through the ventilation shaft had uncovered the lack of ladders. Their only hope was to wait for rescue crews to dig them out. The trapped men were experienced enough as miners to know this could be a lengthy process.

There was water available, some stored in tanks for the drilling machine, dirty and stale, as well as underground streams trickling through the tunnels. The air continued to prove breathable, if unpleasantly hot and humid. But there was little food: two dozen cans, mostly tuna, packaged crackers, a few dozen liters of juice and milk, some leftovers from the men's lunches. They had some illumination from their miners' helmets and the headlights of vehicles stationed down there.

Under the leadership of their foreman, Luis Urzúa, the miners organized themselves for long-term survival, meting out a few mouthfuls of food per day, rationing the light so that they spent much of their time in darkness. The men had plenty of room to move around, since there were several kilometers of unblocked tunnels and chambers outside the emergency shelter. They took turns making loud noises as a signal to the rescue crews. Accustomed to hard labor, they worked to clear away loose rock, improvised a lighting system using truck batteries, and dug channels to divert water from their place of refuge. Just as those on the surface had heard no sounds of life from below, so the men could not hear the sounds of the rescue crews searching for them far above.

As food ran out and their bodies weakened, the men began to despair of rescue. Because of the high humidity, many of the miners were suffering from fungal infections as well as respiratory difficulties from the dust and poor air quality. The mountain continued to creak and groan, periodically releasing fresh rockfalls. Every time it happened, the men feared that their remaining refuge would collapse. When at last they heard the drill approaching, only to pass them by, they became certain they would die in their underground prison.

Many of the miners expressed in their messages how their collective prayer times under the spiritual leadership of José Henríquez had been the decisive factor that kept faith and hope alive until the wonderful moment when the drill broke through at the very edge of their refuge. "God was our thirty-fourth Miner," they repeated over and over.

Two more boreholes were completed down to the miners, allowing for more extensive deliveries and for backups in case problems should develop with any of the shafts. Now that they were receiving food, clean water, medicines, and communication with the outside, the men were rapidly recovering their health. A small video camera had been sent down. On Tuesday, August 31, the trapped miners sent up to the surface a video they'd put together. In the video they showed their living conditions, primitive and meager but well organized.

They also shared in detail their daily living routine. They had divided their time into segments of sleep, work, meals, and games, creating a regular routine that covered the necessary tasks of their daily lives while preventing the boredom so destructive of good mental health. In this way, they had prepared themselves to endure the long wait until Christmas when it was hoped they would be rescued.

The very next day, Wednesday, September 1, the government installed a fiber-optic cable that ran down through one of the boreholes to the emergency shelter, providing digital video communication between the miners and their families as well as with the rescue personnel. The family members deeply appreciated this new instrument of communication which let them converse face to face with the trapped loved ones they had not seen in so long.

On Thursday, September 2, just when the launching of the worldwide prayer chain was scheduled, the camp received a surprise visit from Cardinal Francisco Javier Errázuriz. In its electronic edition for that day, *The Terra News*, a publication of the energy and water industries, made the following comments:

"The cardinal arrived at the airport of Copiapó to visit the place where thirty-three miners have been trapped since August 5, to speak with them by the telephone line that connects the group to the surface, then at 4 p.m., to celebrate a mass with the families and rescue crews."

Cardinal Errázuriz reported later in a news conference, "The miners demonstrate a spirit of hope, solidarity, and much faith, which gives us as well great hope that they will be able to endure until they can be rescued."

He added a reference to our evening prayer vigils. "Every day a time of prayer is held here at the camp for the miners."

The 4 p.m. mass held by the cardinal lasted beyond the time

slot when we usually prayed for the miners and when on this day we'd planned to announce the worldwide prayer chain. But as in every other situation to date, God provided us with a solution. That night the camp was celebrating the birthday of Pía Bognia, wife of mining consultant Miguel Fortt, who had come up with the idea for the *paloma* to supply the trapped miners and whose comments about the white butterfly had been so widely repeated in the press. A Copiapó native with extensive experience in mine rescues, Miguel was beloved by all at Camp Hope for his generous volunteer labor on the San José operation. That night the families of the trapped miners had organized a surprise party for Pía. An outgoing woman, very elegant but always good-humored and kindly, she too had come to be greatly loved by everyone at Camp Hope.

Members of the miner families escorted her with blindfolded eyes to the dining tent along with her husband. She must have guessed something was up, since it was after all her birthday. But she had no idea just who was the distinguished organizer of her surprise party. When Pía's blindfold was removed, Brunilda González stood in front of her. As mayor of Caldera, where the Fortt family had their residence and in whose jurisdiction the San José Mine lies, Mrs. González had organized the entire feast together with the families of the trapped miners.

It was a wonderful party. At the very end, I was pleasantly surprised when the mayor of Caldera turned toward me and asked, "And now, Pastor Parra, what about the prayer chain?"

So right there we held the official inauguration of the worldwide prayer chain. I prayed for Pía, that God would bless her life on this day celebrating her birth. I prayed for the families of the miners that they would be granted patience during the long wait, strength in their uncertainty, assurance in the hope of God's answers to prayer. I prayed for the miners, for their endurance in those dark depths of the mine, for their safety in the midst of so many possible dangers, for the acceleration of the rescue efforts.

Above all, I prayed for the divine gift of time. Who could command the exact timing of the miners' rescue better than God? The technical experts said they would be out by Christmas. But their families needed them out long before then. We couldn't demand of the rescue technicians that they do a faster job, since they were offering the very best scenario they had available. That left God, and He was far more capable than any rescue crew!

I prayed as well for our government authorities, the coordinators of the rescue operation, the rescue crews, and all the different machines that were laboring over the three rescue plans. The spiritual atmosphere there in the tent was intense, as Pía Bognia later described it herself, with an overwhelming sense that God was very real and in control. In those moments of spiritual closeness, we experienced as a group an absolute confidence that God would indeed watch over all thirty-three miners, bringing them out to freedom safely and soundly—and soon.

That night as I drove home to Copiapó, where God had sent me to minister less than two years earlier, I found myself filled with a deep gratitude. I had come to this dry, barren region of the Atacama Desert without ever asking myself why. Each time the leadership of my denomination had transferred me to some new place, I had never hesitated. I had now spent twelve years in pastoral ministry, always going where I was sent with the certainty that this was where God wanted me. My family—Gloria, Carlos

Malaquías, and Belén—had always felt the same way. As a family, we had accepted without question each new move to which the church leadership had assigned us. We knew we were here in Copiapó by the will of God and not our own will.

Now thanks to that fiber-optic cable, the miners trapped deep underground were at this very moment enjoying direct communication with their families far above. Meanwhile we on the surface were able to communicate with our own heavenly Father far above on behalf of the miners through the medium of prayer. As I drove, I felt welling up inside me a great joy at the privilege God had given me to serve Him, a closeness to God and to my brothers and sisters such as we'd experienced as a group during Pía's birthday celebration when we'd come together in unified prayer for the miners, their families, and the rescue teams.

The emotion sweeping over me was so strong that I stopped the car and got out. There on the hard, cracked soil of the desert landscape, a chilly night wind biting into my bones, I raised my hands to heaven, pouring out my thanksgiving to God for the miracle He had brought about in the mine and for all the spiritual blessings He so lovingly bestows upon us as His children.

10

SEPTEMBER,
MONTH OF CELEBRATION AND HOPE

The prayer chain, now operating all around the world, became part of Camp Hope's daily routine every evening at 6 p.m. From below in the mine, José Henríquez informed me that the miners had added a second prayer time themselves at 6 o'clock in order to participate with their families in the worldwide prayer chain.

Meanwhile, Camp Hope had by now become a small city, though far more sophisticated than any normal city of its size. The brown, dusty hilltops around the mine had sprouted Internet, TV, and cable antennas, portable toilets, shower stalls, and other commodities indispensable in such a large camp. Huge television screens offered service to the entire community. There was food prepared by professional hands and all free. Electricity and water were provided without cost to anyone. There was police protection, round-the-clock medical and psychological care, and direct access to municipal, provincial, and national government authorities, including the president himself.

There was also round-the-clock spiritual care, not just from myself as Camp Hope chaplain, but other pastors and Christian volunteers who gave their time freely to help at the camp, hold concerts and activities for both children and adults, and communicate with the trapped miners as well. And if all that weren't enough, God had provided the best rescue team the world had ever put together.

Above all else, there was God Himself in full demonstration of His great power, to whom with absolute confidence we could turn to plead, "Hear our prayers; give us this miracle."

Still, if it had not been for the bicentennial celebrations, which centered around the actual anniversary on September 18, the gloominess of an extended wait would have settled over the camp. And there was another more insidious temptation. The entire country of Chile was celebrating the bicentennial with lots of partying, abundant food, and, above all, large quantities of alcohol, which had its usual consequences of drunken fights and domestic quarrels.

In such crowded confines as Camp Hope, overindulgence could lead to all kinds of trouble. The families of the trapped miners were determined not to let this happen. Rejecting proposals to install refreshment stands selling alcoholic drinks within the camp boundaries, they announced, "We want people to enjoy themselves, but with sobriety. We have our men down in the mine. In view of that situation, we aren't in the mood for any kind of wild carousing."

This became the prevailing tone of Camp Hope for the celebration month. During the first few days of the month, although not much at San José Mine could be described as exactly routine, nothing spectacular happened. Both on the surface and down in the mine, there were occasional differences. But whatever differences arose among the trapped men, few details ever filtered to the surface. They had made among themselves a pact of solidarity and would not talk with outsiders about the negative aspects of their daily lives. A similar pact existed among the families and the rescue crews. If the miners did not want to add to the troubles of the people working so hard on the surface to rescue them, those on the surface didn't want to communicate anything to the miners that might add to the stress of their situation. One consequence in these early days was that letters and communications were carefully monitored in both directions.

By September 6, Plan B using the Schramm T-130 drill was advancing so well that the rescue experts were now talking about pushing forward the likely date of the rescue, possibly even as early as the end of October. On September 12, the Chilean navy shipyards began working on a design to construct three "Phoenix capsules" that could be used to bring the men to the surface once a big enough shaft had been drilled to their location. Each missile-shaped capsule weighed almost half a ton and was just wide enough for a miner to squeeze inside behind a door of heavy steel mesh. If all went well, once the shaft was completed, the Phoenix capsule would be lowered to the miners by means of a powerful industrial winch.

The various bicentennial celebrations scheduled between September 17 and 20 brought three noteworthy visitors to Camp

Hope. First came the Protestant chaplain assigned to La Moneda ("The Coin"), as the president's palace was called, along with numerous Christian leaders. Then came a visit from a group of Adventist youth from across northern Chile. Finally, the president of the Republic, Sebastian Piñera himself, arrived to celebrate the bicentennial with the camp residents.

La Moneda was originally built as a mint for the production of coins during the Spanish colonial era but became the seat of the Chilean government in 1845. Two chaplains, one Catholic and one Protestant, were appointed to the palace by each successive presidential administration. Rev. Alfredo Cooper, a Chilean-born pastor of British descent, had been appointed the Protestant chaplain by President Piñera in January 2010. He arrived at Camp Hope accompanied by Bishop Eduardo Durán, senior pastor of the large Evangelical Cathedral of Santiago, along with Rev. Sergio Soriano, president of the Association of Evangelical Pastors of Copiapó.

Upon arrival, the group headed directly to the site where the three huge drills were working on their three simultaneous plans, A, B, and C, with the intention of videoconferencing with the miners. I wasn't aware of their arrival. But when someone informed me the group was there, I immediately approached them to see if there was any way, as chaplain of Camp Hope, that I could offer them assistance. They asked if they could meet together with all the families.

By this time a large platform had been set up just outside the entrance to the dining tent in an open area, both for news announcements and for public performances from various musical groups who volunteered their services to help entertain the camp residents. At that particular moment, an ensemble specializing in traditional Chilean folk music had just started a concert with the intention of singing thirty-three songs, one for each miner. Since they'd barely commenced their program, this would take some time. But I made arrangements for the visiting pastors to use the music group's sound system once the concert was over to address the families. The concert went well into the evening, so the visiting pastors kept their addresses brief, assuring the families that all the churches of Chile were praying for them and for the trapped miners. The presidential chaplain expressed his own satisfaction to discover that Camp Hope had a pastor serving as chaplain, as he had not been aware that there was one.

From September 16 to 19, at the height of the bicentennial celebration, the Adventist churches of northern Chile held their own youth congress. About seventy young delegates from various area churches, along with a delegation from the Adventist University of Chile in Chillán, were in attendance. For the event, the organizers had rented a beautiful regional country club facility named Allillay about thirty kilometers from Copiapó. This was perhaps the most attractive zone in the region and certainly the greenest, with well-tended lawns, leafy trees, cultivated flower beds, and a sizable swimming pool. The area reminded me of the beautiful green region where I'd grown up in southern Chile but with a big difference. The lush vegetation of southern Chile is natural. Here in the north it is the result of human dedication, since without irrigation and careful tending, the whole place would be pure desert without any vegetation at all.

The youth delegates wanted to do something to help the miners' families only a short drive away at Camp Hope. They hoped to donate some needed supplies or help with some necessary service. So I spoke with the administrators of the two main sectors of Camp Hope activity: those providing necessary daily supplies and those cooking and serving food to the camp residents.

The first sector was under the administration of Alberto Gordillo, general coordinator of the camp. He informed me that if the youth wanted to donate something, the most urgent current need was bottled water and any kind of nonalcoholic drinks. Following his instructions, we looked for a donor to contribute the water. The owner of an area supermarket, Mrs. Walera Tornel, a generous and compassionate woman and a member of one of my church congregations, made a donation to provide the water, around 500 liters in all.

Since among the delegation from the Adventist University was their chamber choir, a concert for the Camp Hope residents seemed an appropriate activity. María Ines, from the nearby town of Caldera, was in charge of the dining tent. I spoke with her about the possibility. I explained to her that the Adventist University, located in Chillán, was an accredited educational institution with a top reputation across Chile, offering some twenty career majors in its four departments: Engineering and Business, Education and Social Sciences, Theology, and Health Sciences. Its student body comes from all over Chile and even from all parts of the world.

Immediately she asked, "Do they sing spiritual and folk music?"

"Yes," I told her.

"Since we're in the middle of the bicentennial celebrations, it would be wonderful if they could sing some folk music. But considering our current circumstances, maybe they had better concentrate on spiritual music."

When the choir bus pulled into Camp Hope for the concert on September 16, each of the forty choir members wore a red jacket, their usual costume but very similar to those used by representatives of Chile's various government departments. Minister of Mines Laurence Golborne was at that very moment in the camp up on the hilltop where the semicircle of Chilean flags were flying, one for each miner. Speaking to Golborne's administrative assistant, I asked if it would be possible to introduce the choir to him when he came down from the knoll. When she agreed, we waited in the bus for the minister's arrival.

Approaching the bus where the choir members waited, Minister Golborne glanced inside at the young people. "And these government jackets?" he commented jokingly. "Where did they get them?"

Following his lead, I joked in return, "The truth is, Minister, that these young people are representatives of the government of heaven."

Their choir director, Susana Ovalle, spoke up. "Minister, it would be a good thing if you would visit our university in Chillán."

"It would be a pleasure," he answered. "Send me the invitation."

Susana Ovalle then invited the minister to attend the concert. He would love to attend, Minister Golborne responded, but he had to leave camp immediately to keep another appointment. As his entourage drove out of camp a short time later, Minister Golborne passed close by where the choir was getting ready. Leaning out the window, he waved good-bye to them.

When the choir began their concert on the platform outside

the dining tent, the place was packed with people. The music they'd chosen was not raucous or frivolous, but majestic, spiritual songs with beautiful harmonies that expressed deep faith, hope, and praise to God. The thunderous applause of the miners' families expressed their appreciation and approval.

The dining tent administrator, María Ines, had informed me earlier that one appropriate contribution our youth could make to the camp would be to help serve food in the dining tent. They needed a crew of ten volunteers to serve tables at each of the three meals: breakfast, lunch, and supper. On Friday, September 17, the day after the concert, the midday meal was a specially prepared feast in honor of the bicentennial celebration. This was served in two shifts, and volunteers from the youth congress served at both.

All the family members of the trapped miners and rescue personnel participated in the meal along with visiting congressmen, senators, and other government officials. At the end of the meal, Chilean senator Isabel Allende gave an address to the group and then asked me to pray for the miners. By this point, all involved in the rescue operation had come to recognize the role that faith played in the lives of the miners and their families. Even those who did not have any personal religious conviction of their own could admit that something extraordinary and miraculous had happened in the rescue operation beyond what they could see and touch. Respect for that spiritual reality was demonstrated in the prayers and acknowledgement of God that accompanied every activity of the camp.

On Sunday, September 19, President Sebastian Piñera visited the camp. After having completed his scheduled appearances in the military parade and other festivities in the capital of Santiago, he'd traveled to Camp Hope to celebrate the bicentennial with the miners' families. This was a previously announced visit. I was helping with the youth congress the day of his scheduled arrival. That morning I went out into the grounds of the Allillay Country Club facility to enjoy the luxuriant vegetation as I spent some time in prayer. The grass and trees, the flowers, and the joyous songs of the birds called up vivid memories of my childhood in the lush green zone of Coelemu, my birthplace.

But present-day reality soon thrust itself back into my thoughts. The scheduled arrival of President Piñera had been a reminder of the Bible that I had dedicated earlier for him but had not been able to deliver due to his sudden departure back to Santiago. Now that he was returning to the mine, I wanted to give the Bible to him, both out of a desire to share God's Word and to express appreciation for his extraordinary participation in the rescue of the miners. But how to do it in a way that would not seem presumptuous or pushy?

There among the leafy, green trees of the country club gardens, I prayed that God Himself would open a door of opportunity to give this Bible to President Piñera. Then in faith I dressed in a formal suit appropriate for an encounter with the president. Seeking out David Gómez, director of education and communication for our denomination in northern Chile, I invited him to come along.

"We're going to try to interview the president and give him this Bible that has been dedicated to him," I told David. "You can bring along your camera and be our photojournalist to record the moment."

He accepted the invitation, and we went. Since the Allillay facility was close to San José Mine, it didn't take us long to arrive. But though we had no problem entering Camp Hope, the area where the president was meeting with the miners' families had been cordoned off.

"Just the families," I was told by Christian Jahn, the same regional secretary who had earlier forbidden me entrance into the evening briefings. I tried to show him my chaplain credentials that the camp authorities had given me on that earlier occasion.

"That is only for the 6 p.m. assembly," he told me before I could say a word.

At that very moment engineer Miguel Fortt walked up to attend the meeting with the president. Taking in my suit, he greeted me with a smiling comment. "Very elegant!"

"Yes," I answered, "but I'm not allowed inside."

"Wait here," he said. "Let me see what I can do."

A short time later, Angélica Álvarez, the wife of trapped miner Edison Peña, arrived. It was Angélica who had resolved with this same official my earlier difficulty gaining entrance to the daily briefings with the miners' families at 6:00 each evening. Upon her inquiry, I explained why I was not entering the tent. She too promised to do something. A few minutes before the president was scheduled to arrive, Angélica came back to the entrance and said to the regional secretary, "The families would like to pray during our wait for the president, and we require the presence of our chaplain, Pastor Parra."

Without any further objections, I was allowed to enter. My companion, David Gómez, remained outside and was directed to an area where the entire press corps had been assigned to await the president's arrival. This meant he would not be able to take pictures as he'd hoped of the president receiving his Bible. But that was hardly important compared to the delivery of the Bible itself.

I stayed beside Angélica as the families gathered. We prayed together. By then an idea had come to me. I told the others, "I have with me a Bible, like the one each of you received, that has been dedicated to the president. If you are all in agreement, I would like to present it as a gift from the entire group when President Piñera arrives."

I read aloud the inscription in the Bible. They all enthusiastically approved the idea. Angélica herself was to give a short speech to the president and to present a letter on behalf of the miners' shift that had been working near the entrance on the day of the collapse and so had managed to escape. They had not been paid in all these weeks and were going through as many hardships as the families of the trapped miners themselves.

"I'm nervous," she told me. "Please pray to God for me, that I might speak the right words to the president." I promised that I would and that God would be with her to carry out her own mission.

President Piñera's helicopter was now arriving. Stepping down, the president and his entourage headed directly toward where the families, engineers, and rescue personnel were now gathered outside the dining tent along with the government officials handling the mine disaster. Angélica stood at the very front of the group to give her speech. Since I was at her side, I found myself only a short distance from the president. President Piñera greeted the group and wished the families a happy bicentennial.

He reassured them of the government's commitment to rescue the miners and gave an encouraging report regarding the progress of the rescue operation.

When the president finished, Angélica stepped forward to give her own speech. She did so with complete serenity and aplomb and then presented the miners' letter to the president. Accepting the letter, President Piñera immediately turned away. He was headed toward the gathered news crews when one of the family members spoke up.

"President, we have something else to present to you. A gift."

The president stopped. He indicated for us to proceed. On behalf of all the families, I presented the Bible to him. He opened it to the dedicatory inscription while I explained that we were presenting him with this Bible, just as we'd sent down the thirty-three mini-Bibles to the miners, both in celebration of the bicentennial and in recognition of all that President Piñera had done for the miners and of his own role in the miracle God had accomplished.

With clear emotion, President Piñera gave a short speech, thanking the families for the gift before heading over toward the pack of journalists. As for the commemorative photos I'd already dismissed as no longer possible, these ended up multiplied many times over since many of the family members present had cameras and took far more pictures than David Gómez could have done.

The miners themselves celebrated the bicentennial in their own fashion, which we were all able to witness by means of the videoconference feed. This was limited, since there wasn't much space below or any way of getting much of a feast down to them.

But they sang the national anthem, danced some traditional Chilean folk dances, ate a special meal sent to them by means of the *paloma*, and opened gifts from their family members, among them the Chilean flag, which was being flown all over the country in tribute to this special national holiday.

11

EXPECTATIONS AND HOPE

The story of all that happened at San José Mine would lose some of its human and emotional side if it did not include two significant events that occurred in the month of September, one dealing with life, the other with technology. One was the birth of a daughter to trapped miner Ariel Ticona. The other was a third breakdown of the Schramm T-130, the heavy-duty drilling rig being used in Plan B that had now taken the lead in efforts to reach the miners.

Who understands the value of human life better than a person about to lose it—or about to gain it? The thirty-three trapped miners lived both of these in a single experience. When the mine collapse occurred, they came close to losing their lives, and that danger repeated itself often during the weeks of their captivity. When they were rescued, they experienced the joy of being given a new life as they once again set foot outside the mine. But none of the miners experienced the true value of human life more intensely and with greater joy than one single trapped miner, Ariel Ticona.

I know Héctor Ticona, Ariel's father, well, since he is a member of one of the churches that make up my pastoral district, located in Francisco de Aguirre, a suburb of Copiapó. He had come up to the mine to be near his son during the rescue operation. One day I was eating supper with him in the big dining tent when he showed me a letter he'd received from his son. Correspondence between the miners and their family members was now circulating smoothly by means of the *paloma*, the 7.5-centimeter-wide pipe by which supplies traveled through the narrow borehole from the surface to the bottom of the mine.

Ariel Ticona's first child, a daughter, was due to be born in September. A young couple very much in love, Ariel and his wife Elizabeth Segovia were eagerly awaiting the arrival of a child into their home. By the time the mine collapse trapped the thirty-three men, Ariel and Elizabeth had already chosen a name for their daughter: Carolina Elizabeth.

Now Ariel's father, Héctor, informed me excitedly, "Ariel's wife Elizabeth is due to deliver a daughter any day now. Ariel wants to change the name they've chosen. Instead of Carolina Elizabeth, as they'd planned to call her, he wants to name their daughter Esperanza Elizabeth."

A couple days later, Héctor approached me. "My daughter-in-law has agreed. They are going to call her Esperanza."

Little Esperanza was born on September 14, 2010. Since Elizabeth Segovia had delivered the baby at a regional clinic in Copiapó, I went to pay her a pastoral visit. Arriving at the clinic, I took note of the numerous media teams surrounding the facility, their large video cameras busily filming. Among them I recognized several I'd encountered up at Camp Hope—CNN, a Chinese news agency, and a Spanish journalist who had interviewed me on an earlier occasion.

"I suppose you are all here for the birth of Ariel Ticona's daughter," I commented to the Spanish journalist.

"It is a great news story," he responded.

It was undoubtedly a great news story. There are those who consider it to be the most significant family drama of the entire 69 days that the thirty-three miners spent trapped underground. I had to wait a short time until a foreign journalist finished interviewing Elizabeth. When I first entered the room, it was to an uncomfortable situation. Though many of Ariel's family members were up at Camp Hope, because of her late-stage pregnancy and on medical advice, Elizabeth had not traveled to the mine at all. And although I knew well her father-in-law and many of her extended family, I had not personally met Ariel's wife before this time. Since I had been serving as a press representative for Radio Nuevo Tiempo as well as camp chaplain, I happened to have a small camera hanging around my neck. So when I entered the room, she reacted with dismay. She would talk to no more members of the press, she announced heatedly.

"It's okay, I am the chaplain of Camp Hope," I reassured her. "I am your father-in-law's pastor and the one who sent a miniature Bible down to your husband so that he might have spiritual encouragement during the long wait that the rescue is going to take."

"Oh yes, of course, Pastor," Elizabeth responded at once. "I've heard all about you. I'm so sorry; I thought you were another one of those journalists."

I prayed with Elizabeth that God would bless her precious new baby girl and her husband down in the mine and that they would soon be united as a family. Thanks to the fiber-optic video connection the Chilean government had installed, the baby's father, Ariel Ticona, as well as the rest of the miners, were able to witness little Esperanza's first moments of life. There was a joyous celebration, both on the surface at Camp Hope and 700 meters deep down into the rock. There further avalanches, darkness, and hunger remained a constant peril for the trapped miners. But for this day, the new father and his companions celebrated this living testimony to the hope that sustained each heart.

In the midst of this celebration of new life, the Schramm T-130 drill, so central to the success of Plan B, had already begun to enlarge one of the original boreholes to a shaft 71 centimeters (28 inches) in diameter in order to raise the miners to the surface. But just a few days later, on September 22, the drill suffered its third breakdown since the rig had started drilling less than three weeks earlier.

The manufacturer of the Schramm drill is a North American company that has been based in Pennsylvania since the year 1900. But only since 2001 had they begun manufacturing this particular class of drills. In the entire world, only 115 of the T-130 drills exist. Three of those were already in Chile, two of them already moved to the San José Mine for the rescue operation. The drill had already been successfully used for a mine rescue eight years earlier in Quecreek, Pennsylvania, but at only one-tenth the depth at which the thirty-three Chilean miners were trapped.

The Plan B Schramm T-130 drill had begun drilling on Sunday, September 5. In four days, up to Wednesday, September 8, it had advanced 268 meters. Then it had to stop for fourteen hours to change some cables. This was the first breakdown.

A second, more serious breakdown occurred on September 9. The drill had slammed into a length of metal tubing and broken off the drill head, which now lay hundreds of meters down the deep shaft, blocking any further progress. An attempt was made to pull the metal chunks out with huge magnets, but to no avail.

Then a young Chilean engineer, Igor Proestakis, only twenty-four years old and the nephew of one of the lead rescue engineers, Mijail Proestakis, designed an ingenious apparatus he named "the spider." Similar to a medieval-era bear trap, this was a circular metal device with eight curved metal claws that looked much like spider legs. Once lowered to the bottom of the shaft, the spider's legs would be closed around the broken drill pieces like a trap springing shut so that the rescue team could pull them back to the surface. The operation was tricky, and the rescue team could not be sure whether they would be able to pull the broken metal to the surface or might even have to start over again with a new shaft.

At any rate, the drilling would be halted for at least twenty-four hours. In the face of this new setback, both miners and families reacted with renewed anxiety. Down at Camp Hope, it was clear from the silence that drilling on the hilltop had ceased.

Minister of Mines Laurence Golborne responded quickly to the families' worries. "I have been told that a lot of you are expressing deep concern, and we understand your worries. But understand that the stopping and starting of the drills is a normal part of the process. There is nothing out of the ordinary happening at this time. These machines have to stop constantly for repairs and to rest the equipment, and some of the other machines are currently stopped because we are dealing at this moment with Plan B. That is precisely why we have three distinct plans so that if one produces a technical difficulty, we can move to another. We are working in parallel with all three plans to insure that the rescue takes place in the shortest time possible."

Sure enough, after a three-day delay and the successful use of the spider, Plan B started up once more and once again took the lead. By September 22, it had finished the first stage of widening the borehole from its original 14 centimeters (5.5 inches) to 30 centimeters (12 inches). This borehole was not the original one that had broken through to the miners at their emergency shelter; the new shaft terminated at a workshop located in a tunnel about fifty meters higher than the level where the miners had taken refuge. The choice of location was to ensure that if any difficulties arose from the drilling, the tunnel where the miners were located would not be affected.

With the borehole widened to 30 centimeters, the final shaft was now being drilled, widening the shaft further to 71 centimeters (28 inches) in diameter, which would allow passage of the Phoenix capsule. This widened shaft had been completed to less than 100 meters in depth when the drill broke down again. This time a large piece of the drill head tumbled down the shaft, landing in the tunnel below.

At the bottom of the shaft, the trapped miners had been working steadily to clear away the debris of the drilling as it fell through into the tunnel. Falling such a distance, the broken drill head weighed more than enough to cause serious injury if it struck one of the miners. The families of Camp Hope learned of the incident only through the media coverage being shown on television screens around the camp. But the news reports said nothing about the result of this chunk of metal falling among the miners. The families raised angry protests.

Once again, the Schramm T-130 was at a standstill for replacement of the drill head. Minister Golborne and André Sougarret, the engineer in charge of the rescue, held a meeting with the miner families. Visibly worried, but also irritated, the family members grumbled, "How can you give news like this of a breakdown to the media crews, and to us, the families, you say nothing? You need to give news first of all to the families and only then to the press."

The rescue officials offered an apology. "We didn't give the information to the press. It somehow leaked. Please excuse this unfortunate incident. From now on we will try to be more careful about this type of leak. You will always be the first ones informed when we have new information, followed by the press. And you don't need to worry about the miners being hurt, because everything we are doing is in direct coordination with them. The removal of debris isn't going on while the drill is working, but only after it stops. Only when their safety has been secured do they come in with an earthmover that was stationed in that part of the tunnel when the mine collapse occurred."

Along with their worries for the physical well-being of the miners, the families were also anxious for the state of the Schramm T-130 drill itself. And there had been breakdowns of the other two drills as well, both of them already far behind the

Schramm T-130. Could any of these breakdowns permanently paralyze the rescue efforts?

André Sougarret explained to the Camp Hope residents that they had two Schramm T-130 drills. Even if one completely broke down, they would still be able to continue with the other. With the situation resolved and the families reassured that no miner had been injured, drilling resumed the next day, continuing to widen the shaft to the diameter necessary for the final rescue.

Despite its limitations and breakdowns, the technology available to the rescue crews was completing its task with admirable efficiency, thanks to the careful planning and skill of its operators. But the very evident hand of an Almighty Providence was also acknowledged at every moment of the rescue operation.

12

COMIC RELIEF

Life at Camp Hope and down in the mine had now settled into a routine of *paloma* deliveries, work, drilling, and waiting. Reports from the medical personnel and psychologists monitoring the trapped miners indicated that they were recovering health and strength. But always at the back of everyone's mind was the uncertainty whether all this massive effort would be successful in the end.

No one had ever rescued miners trapped at such a depth, and many things could go wrong. One major concern was the continued tremors that occasionally shook the mountain. The men below were kept busy clearing away newly fallen rock slabs. One single large-scale tremor or another "sitting" of the mountain, and all the rescue efforts to this point could be wiped out in a moment.

So the mood both at Camp Hope and in the mine was always serious and sometimes despairing as new setbacks arose. Yet there were moments as well of fun and even hilarity—especially once another new guest arrived at the camp. He was a very simple personage, his only interest in helping people, especially children. Of ordinary size, even small, his features were round and plump, with a bright red nose perched like a large cherry in the middle of a snowy complexion. His dress was unusual for Camp Hope visitors: bright yellow baggy pants trimmed in neon orange, a baggy shirt of mixed orange and black, a sky-blue vest, and everything topped off by a sky-blue cap.

Yes, Rolly the Clown had arrived at Camp Hope!

His actual name was Rolando González. Rolly was a native of Iquique, a sizable city that is capital of Chile's northernmost region on the Pacific coast not far from the Peruvian border. But he arrived at Camp Hope on September 12, from the mining town of Calama, near Antofagasta, where he worked for a construction firm that did contract assignments for an area mining company. His gentle, comical humor and mischievous pranks immediately endeared him to Camp Hope children and adults alike.

Rolly had originally left his own full-time job to offer his vacation days during the bicentennial celebration to the families of the trapped miners. So when the bicentennial festivities ended on September 19, the clown came to the families to announce his return to his own regular job. The reaction of the camp's children was immediate and strong. Tears streaming as they hugged Rolly, they begged, "Please, just stay a few more days."

When Rolly explained that he had to leave, the children searched out Minister of Mines Laurence Golborne. Surrounding the minister, they began chanting, "We want him to stay! We want him to stay!"

Minister Golborne asked Rolly what arrangements would be necessary for the clown to stay on until the rescue had been completed. An agreement was reached with his employers, and Rolly stayed on, becoming the official "clown of Camp Hope." He spent his time with the children from morning until evening, playing with them and cheering them up. Learning of his kindness through messages sent to them by family members, the miners decided to show their gratitude by sending up to Rolly a large Chilean flag that had been lowered down into the mine for their own bicentennial celebration, autographed by each of the miners.

Rolly the Clown's spirit of kindness and generosity was never more evident than when a Christian singing group visited the camp October 5 to hold a concert. The Asaf Quartet, an all-male quartet from Santiago, was comprised of a father, Gabriel Bernal Torres, and his three sons, Gabriel, Jonatán, and Dany Bernal. Organized as a group in the year 2000, Asaf had by this time held concerts all over Chile and abroad in Argentina, Brazil, Bolivia, Peru, Ecuador, Colombia, Switzerland, and the UK. The quartet held their concert on the platform built for the camp's public activities just outside the dining tent. Their program included inspirational numbers geared to both adults and children. At the end they gave one of their music CDs to each of the thirty-three miner families.

Rolly the Clown, visibly touched by the spiritual message of the music, especially the songs for children, improvised a ceremony of appreciation for the quartet. Inviting onto the platform some of the camp leadership, including Brunilda González, mayor of Caldera; Liliana, the wife of one of the trapped miners; and María Segovia, Camp Hope's "mayor," Rolly emerged in his clown costume with a black knapsack over his shoulder. From the knapsack he took out a folded Chilean flag. To everyone's surprise when he unfolded it, they saw that it was the flag which the thirty-three miners had autographed and sent up to the surface as a gift to him.

Displaying the flag to the audience, he then offered it as a gift to the visiting quartet. For once, there was no comedy in his gestures, just a sincere and kindly generosity that deeply touched the quartet as well as the crowd. Through his unselfish action captured on film and shared with a watching world, Rolly metamorphosed from being a simple camp clown into an inspirational symbol of generosity and selflessness that lifted the hearts not only of the Camp Hope residents but of all Chile during those last anxious days of the rescue operation.

There were others whose kindness and generosity deserve full mention. Among these was a team from the National Aeronautics and Space Administration, or NASA, the American space agency, who traveled out to San José Mine soon after the miners were discovered alive. Since the NASA experts were experienced at handling issues of isolation, close confinement, and difficult living conditions for astronauts in space, from the beginning they helped lay out daily routines and necessary strategies to maintain physical and mental health among the trapped miners. Part of the protocol set up under the advice of the NASA experts was a system of lighting, twelve hours of light and twelve of dark, that restored a sense of normal daytime and nighttime to the miners. They also helped with the design of the Phoenix capsules, which the Chilean navy was building to raise the miners 700 meters to the surface once the rescue shaft was completed.

Two men who oversaw the implementation of NASA suggestions were the chief medical officer for the rescue operation, Dr. Jean Romagnoli, and psychologist Dr. Alberto Iturra. Dr. Romagnoli is a specialist in the field of sports trauma. During the rescue mission, he was in charge of one of the three *paloma* stations.

Dr. Romagnoli explained his work: "In my station we carried out a series of diverse functions such as daily medical checks of the trapped miners, logistics operations, and monitoring of air quality in the mine. This station was the only physical communication with the interior of the mine. Each day we had to send down the daily necessities of the miners, a difficult task considering we were dealing with a hole only 8.5 inches in diameter (slightly wider than the first borehole, which was only 7.5 centimeters). Despite these challenges, we managed to send down even camping mattresses. The most difficult issue was the temperature in the interior of the mine, over 30 degrees C (90° F), which turned their entire living quarters into a sauna type atmosphere, making any prolonged activity for the men very difficult." One of the solutions implemented was the piping of refrigerated oxygen into the emergency refuge, helping to lower the temperatures to a slightly more tolerable level.

Dr. Iturra, a psychologist from nearby Calera, oversaw the mental health of the miners, spending an hour in videoconference with them every day at 3 p.m. A cautious man, he supervised every detail related to the miners' daily routine to avoid anything that might provoke undesired emotions or negatively affect their spirits. This was not easy, and there were often clashes between the psychologist and the miners as well as their families over issues such as censoring news from the surface.

Both men were doing outstanding work under very difficult circumstances, and by the end had developed a close relationship with the miners and their families. I came to know Dr. Romagnoli and Dr. Iturra well during my weeks at the camp, since as the camp chaplain I felt a responsibility for the spiritual well-being of the miners and worked alongside the two doctors to communicate with the miners underground. A special blessing was to communicate with José Henríquez, who continued to be a strong spiritual leader among the miners, serving as their own personal pastor in the depths of the mine.

13

VIGILS OF HOPE

By Friday, September 24, the miners had been underground fifty days, the longest such recorded captivity in mining history. On September 25, the Phoenix capsules arrived at the San José Mine from the Chilean naval shipyard where they had been built. A field clinic was set up to give immediate medical attention once the miners were out. Police reinforcements arrived to provide added security during the final rescue operation.

By the beginning of October, a fresh spirit of hope and optimism had taken hold of Camp Hope. All three plans were advancing, the precarious structure of the mine had to this point maintained a necessary stability, and hope was now high that the rescue operation had reached its closing stages. By Monday, October 4, Plan B had reached almost 600 meters into the mountain. The next day, a rescue team of fourteen specialists was chosen to descend into the mine to help the miners with the ascent when the time came.

But the rescue authorities could make no concrete promises. The miners' families witnessed the extra flurry of activity with joy, but it was a contained joy. There had already been great setbacks when everything seemed to appear promising, dating back to that first terrible blow when the probe completely missed the miners, through all the various breakdowns of drills and other equipment. Another setback was always possible. No one dared speculate what it could be. There could be rockslides that would put an end to the current operation or even a complete breakdown of the Schramm T-130 and other backup drills. No one wanted to consider such a possibility, but everyone feared it.

On October 7, while the T-130 drill was idle for scheduled maintenance, María Segovia once again gave evidence of her strong spiritual leadership as she approached me to suggest, "Pastor Parra, while we are waiting for the T-130 to break through the final distance to the miners, why don't we as an entire camp implement our own special vigil of prayer and song in addition to the worldwide prayer chain?"

Up to that point, we had been gathering every evening at 6 p.m. to pray. That evening after I'd given my usual devotional talk and prayed for continued endurance and hope for both the miners and their families, María came up front to address the group. "Friends, we need to pray even more fervently now that the moment of the rescue is close at hand. So Pastor Carlos Parra here is going to lead us in a vigil, praying and singing together all through the night and day until the drill reaches the bottom and we can bring our boys up."

Her leadership was so well respected in the group that the others immediately agreed to the idea. For myself, it was a great delight to be able to contribute to such a wonderful spiritual experience.

"You invite the people," I told María, "and I will make arrangements for a big group bonfire and a team of musicians to help with worship music. I'll also choose some appropriate Bible texts to read. We can pray, sing, and read God's Word together."

"That sounds wonderful, Pastor," María responded. "I'll do my part."

When God's hand is on our plans, things come together better than anything we ourselves can possibly arrange. I had invited Claudio Belmar, a professor of music at the Adventist University in Chillán, to join us. He arrived at Camp Hope with a full team of musicians, each bringing their instruments, including guitars and trumpets, along with a portable sound system. We were able to raise a large overhead screen where we projected the words of the songs so everyone could join in. At the very entrance into San José Mine where the narrow, winding road curves sharply one last time and then opens up onto the camp, we lit thirty-three candles, one for each miner. If only symbolically, we had the miners present with us. The small, wavering flames of the candles were shaped like two hands placed together in an attitude of prayer. With that symbol of steady, shining light in the darkness of the desert night, we were expressing our faith and hope for the safe rescue of all the miners.

That night about 150 people gathered for the vigil around the large bonfire we'd built. These included family members of the miners, journalists, mayors, senators, other politicians, and

volunteers. We sang worship songs and fun action choruses for
the children. We divided into small groups of six to ten people to
pray. We all joined hands and prayed in turn for each one of the
miners. Participants in the vigil led out in prayer for each other,
for all the different families and what they were going through,
and for what was happening down in the mine.

Above all, we prayed to God that the drilling would continue its current accelerated pace. From the day that the miners
had been found alive, we'd been praying that the time of their
captivity would be reduced, that they would not have to stay in
the mine until Christmas as the technical experts had originally
estimated. Already they had been down there longer than any
trapped miner had ever survived. To wait another two months or
more in that terrible heat and humidity was too much.

"Lord God, heavenly Father," we prayed, "please shorten their
stay. Shorten it a lot. We know that You are capable of increasing
the efficiency of the machines and all the different technology.
Bless the drilling rigs so that they will hold up under such intense
labor and so many hours of continuous use."

During that night of vigil, we prayed the same plea over and
over in many different forms. We prayed together, we sang, we
played Bible games, and we shared testimonies of our own faith
and hope, both together as a group and in conversations during
the breaks between group sessions. It was truly a very special night.
We could feel God's presence within our own hearts, among us as
a group, and all around us in nature itself.

The desert nights are not in general pleasurable or attractive.
Most nights in that area, the heavy mist northern residents call
camanchaca rises off the ocean and drifts inland to settle, white

and chill, into the valleys that run through the maze of hills. This nocturnal fog becomes so thick that it is hard to see a meter in front of one's eyes, and the humidity is strong enough to penetrate the warmest clothing to lay clammy, ice-cold fingers against the skin.

But the night of our prayer vigil turned out to be a spectacularly beautiful night. It wasn't as cold as past nights, so that the bonfire was enough to offer a comfortable warmth. There was no *camanchaca*. Instead, high above us, the immense, black expanse of the desert sky twinkled with the bright heavenly lights of the constellations. In those brilliantly jewelled patterns, we could sense the immeasurably greater eternal and infinite light of their Almighty Creator.

"Can't you feel it? God is here with us!" people were exclaiming all around me. "Just look! Have you ever seen a more beautiful night? God is here! God is here!"

A feeling of tremendous peace passed contagiously from person to person throughout the group, a peace as quiet and restful and serene as the dark desert landscape stretching silently away from us under the placid glitter of the stars. In daylight, this same landscape was barren and ugly and broken without a hint of vegetation. But on that clear, bright night, cloaked only by the soft silver-gray of starlight, it held a mystical beauty. All around me in the circle as we sang and prayed, I could see beaming from faces a deep spiritual joy and confidence in God.

I asked aloud, "Would anyone like to volunteer to pray for us all as a group?"

The mayor of nearby Ballenar, Cristian Tapia, immediately spoke up. "Pastor, I'd like to pray."

A number of others gathered close around him to add their support. As he began to pray, emotion choked the mayor's voice. When he finished, he added, "I feel the presence of God here. This is a very special night."

Members of the press corps were also participating in the prayer vigil. At some point, they decided this was a story worth communicating to their audience. All around us, news crews were filming the event. Others were offering live reports. Close by me, I heard one of them speaking into a microphone. "They are holding a prayer vigil up here at Camp Hope. You can just feel that something extraordinary is happening in this place."

Midnight came and went. Showing a considerate respect for this communal spiritual experience, the media crews had taken care not to interrupt the vigil or try to hold interviews. But around 1 a.m., when there was a break in the activities, a news crew approached to ask if I would be willing to transmit a live interview. I was happy to agree. There was nothing particularly formal about the prayer vigil. If we could take breaks to play games and do calisthenics to warm ourselves and cheer everyone up, or sit around chatting companionably between prayer sessions, we could certainly take a moment to accede to these journalists' courteous requests. By doing so, we could also share our prayer vigil with others who might still be up at this hour across Chile as well as around the world.

"What is your main prayer request to God this night?" a reporter asked me.

"We are praying that the Schramm T-130 will soon reach the refuge where the miners have taken shelter without any additional delays," I answered, "and that the capsule being created to extract them can be installed safely to begin the rescue of each and every miner."

By 3 a.m. Thursday, October 7, the crowd gradually began to diminish as people drifted away to their tents to sleep. The prayer vigil continued nevertheless until 9 a.m. By that hour only about thirty people were still praying.

The sense of expectation and hope, however, had not diminished. For that same day, October 7, Minister of Mines Laurence Golborne announced a general rehearsal of the entire planned extraction procedure, step by step. Based on the progress of Plan B the day before, the minister also announced that if all went well, it was hoped that the Schramm T-130 would reach the miners on Saturday, October 9. From the moment that announcement was made, the expectation of everyone in the camp was that the drill might break through to the miners at any moment. That night, to keep ourselves from being distracted or asleep at the moment the drill reached its objective, we continued on with the prayer vigil of the night before. The night of Friday, October 8, we did the same.

On Saturday, October 9, at 8:00 in the morning, the Schramm T-130 drill broke through to where the thirty-three miners had been trapped since August 5. They had now endured two months and four days without seeing a ray of sunlight. The clanging of a bell that preceded every official announcement rang out insistently across the camp. Then the cheers rose up that had been raised so many times during the last two months:

"Chi-chi-chi! Le-le-le! Viva Chile! Long live the miners of Chile!"

Every family member, every rescue crew member and equipment operator, all the camp authorities and volunteers took up the joyous chant. The euphoria of the moment was uncontain-able. How could it not be? Was it not for this very day that all these people had endured the discomfort of their tiny tents, the intense heat of the desert days, the bone-chilling cold of the nights, the anguished delay of the first seventeen days when no one knew whether the miners were dead or alive? How could they not now overflow with wild joy when they had been beg-ging God day and night with expectant faith and hope for this day to come?

And now God had abundantly answered those prayers. After their long weeks of unstinting labor, the technicians, mechanics, and other rescue personnel were as invested emotionally in this moment as the families themselves, and they participated in the celebration with the same euphoria and tears of relief, embracing each other and raising their own cheers of triumph. Down at the bottom of the mine, the thirty-three certainly felt the joy and celebration no less than those of us on the surface. Ecstatic, they poured out their sentiments of gratitude and relief. And not just to the rescue crews. All expressed their gratitude to God for the miracle of this day.

The family members did not forget God either in their joy. We gathered in our usual assembly place beside the dining hall. From that site I led a prayer of gratitude. It was a responsive prayer session with the entire crowd joining in, the families, res-cue workers, camp volunteers, and journalists. The prayer of the entire group took the form of a deeply moving dialogue.

I prayed, "Lord God, we give You thanks."

"We give You thanks," the crowd responded.

"For preserving the lives of all thirty-three miners."

"For preserving the lives of all thirty-three miners," they repeated.

"For permitting all the men to be found."

"For permitting all the men to be found," the crowd recited.

"Now we pray that You will bless the rescue."

"Now we pray that You will bless the rescue," they repeated.

"That we will soon have each of these loved ones with us."

"That we will soon have each of these loved ones with us."

The repetition of each line reverberated through the camp like a deep, solemn echo that was a profound expression of our supreme gratitude to God, who had made this moment possible. When we finished the prayer, I invited the group to climb the hillside to the top of the knoll where the semicircle of Chilean flags, representing each of the miners, waved in the wind. There were actually thirty-four flags up on the knoll, the extra one perhaps left over from when the authorities had thought there were thirty-four miners trapped below.

Or was it such a simple coincidence? Perhaps that extra unmarked flag was there to represent the "thirty-fourth Miner" as the trapped men kept insisting, the Almighty Creator, the God of the universe, who had been in their midst from the beginning. The loving heavenly Father who had guided that small white butterfly to prevent the death of two of the miners; who had directed that drill head toward the roof of the tunnel when it was drifting off course and would have missed the refuge one more time; who through the pages of a Bible only seven centimeters across had expressed His own direct words of comfort and love to the miners during their long ordeal.

Up there on the top of the knoll, we celebrated again. We sang the national anthem. We offered the national pledge of allegiance. We sang songs of praise to God. We commemorated the sixty-five days that had now passed since the mine collapse August 5. Above all, we rejoiced because only three or four days—at most, a week—remained until we would witness the liberation of all thirty-three men trapped for so long in the depths of San José Mine.

14

THE FINAL VIGIL

The T-130 drill had now completed its mission. No longer needed, it was immediately dismantled and prepared for withdrawal from San José Mine. As the convoy carrying all its equipment headed down the hill from the mine, the residents of Camp Hope stood along the road, cheering its passage with loud appreciation.

Up at the drill site, there were new topics of conversation. Would it be necessary to encase in metal tubing the entire length of the newly widened shaft to protect the Phoenix capsule as it descended and ascended? If that proved necessary, how long would such a task take? How much longer could the rescue operation be extended without seriously compromising the health of the miners or risking new avalanches that could damage the finished shaft? Prolonging the rescue efforts through excessive precautions could prove as dangerous as moving too quickly.

The rescue coordinators made the decision to encase only the first ninety meters of the shaft. The lower levels were an extremely solid rock, even harder than ordinary granite. While this had been a problem to the drilling rigs, now it provided insurance that the shaft would not crumble during the raising of the miners. In any case, further creaking within the mountain was causing new alarm among the miners and their rescue crews. There was now a sense of urgency that the men must be extracted without any further delay.

After these decisions, the rescue preparations went forward with great speed. Once the removal of the Schramm T-130 drill was complete, the next step was the installation of the platform from which the Phoenix capsule would be winched down to the miners. Medical personnel stood ready at the field clinic to whisk the miners away on stretchers for an initial health examination. Helicopters were on standby to ferry them to a nearby hospital. Police patrolled the area to keep out sightseers.

Down below, the miners too were getting ready. Green waterproof jumpsuits had been sent down for each, since there was a lot of moisture in the rescue shaft. The Oakley company, manufacturer of high-quality sunglasses, donated a pair for each miner because their eyes would be very sensitive to light after so many weeks underground. Keepsakes the miners wanted to save from their time down below, especially gifts and letters they'd received, were sent up in the *paloma*.

The miners prepared a landing pad for the capsule. Most important was a widening of the landing zone so that there would be room for maneuvering around the Phoenix capsule. Blasting away a piece of wall was an easy task for the experienced miners. But as they did so, the resulting explosion sent tremors through the mountain, triggering rockslides and water seepage along the tunnel. Once again there was a panic among the miners. On the very verge of rescue, after all the work involved, would the mountain finally succeed in killing them all? Some were convinced that they had never been intended to get out. Death was inevitable, and the mountain was just toying with them.

José Henríquez, their spiritual leader, called on the men to have faith. God had not brought them this far to abandon them now. Omar Reygadas, one of the men who had helped José Henríquez provide spiritual leadership to the others, shared afterwards, "To me it was a warning."

God had done a miracle to save them all, Omar went on to say. The miners had been given a second chance at life. They had all made promises to follow God and be better people in the future if they were rescued. Now God was reminding them that they needed to keep their word.

By Tuesday afternoon, October 12, the mountain had quieted down, and the go-ahead was given. A trial run of the Phoenix capsule was executed with a video camera attached so that the engineers could judge its performance and any obstacles it might encounter along the way. The trial run went flawlessly. Once it had returned to the surface, Minister of Mines Laurence Golborne announced, "There was no shaking or rockfall, not even dust. The filming proved everything is in place. The capsule worked well. We will begin the rescue process on Wednesday at zero hours."

Zero hours corresponds to midnight between October 12 and 13. That night we held the last prayer vigil with the family members of the miners. The prayer vigil lasted from midnight on October 12 to midnight October 13 when the last miner emerged. Its objective was very specific: asking God that the rescue operation would be completed without incident and with every miner safely free.

We held the final prayer vigil in front of the tents of María Segovia and her closest neighbor Andrea, wife of trapped miner Claudio Yañez. A group of María's friends had traveled all the way from Antofagasta, 500 kilometers away, where María lived. Devout Christians, they all joined us for the prayer vigil. As was María's usual practice with the intense cold of the desert night, she'd set up a table with hot drinks: coffee, tea, herbal infusions. These were constantly replenished for anyone passing by to serve themselves.

A huge concentration of journalists had arrived to document the final rescue, more than 1600 in all representing at least 500 media outlets. They were not allowed up close to the rescue preparations, so they circulated constantly through the camp. Many stopped by the prayer vigil, pausing briefly to participate in the singing, prayers, Bible readings, and devotional meditations—and of course to carry out their primary task: reporting the events of this night. They filmed the activities of the prayer vigil group, gathered around a bonfire that burned high in front of the two tents. When they could find someone to talk, they filmed a live interview.

At one point a British journalist approached the hot drinks table. He was well dressed, courteous in manner, and friendly. But he didn't speak a word of Spanish. He said questioningly, "English?"

No one attending the drinks table spoke any English. I had learned a little, a very little, but enough for the two of us to understand each other.

"How much is the coffee?" the journalist asked.

Trying to inject a little humor into the cold night, I said jokingly, "Ten dollars a cup."

With unruffled good nature, the man began searching his pockets for ten dollars. Laughing, the nearest bystanders called out, "It's a gift. It doesn't cost anything."

I explained to him with a smile, "No, really, thanks to the generosity of so many people, nothing here is for sale. It is all a free gift. Serve yourself all the coffee you would like—or tea or some other drink if you prefer."

My English isn't very good, but he understood it well enough because he too joined in the laughter as he served himself a hot drink.

During a break in the prayer vigil activities, while some of the group were sitting around singing and others chatting, a German journalist showed up. He only spoke his own language, no Spanish at all. None of us spoke a word of German. But he seemed very interested in what we were doing. Part of our group had used the break time to make some small crepes, similar to tortillas, and were toasting them over the fire. The German journalist immediately began filming a live news release of the scene.

We found the German journalist as charming and interesting as he evidently found us, since we couldn't understand anything he was saying and had to try to make ourselves understood by hand gestures. We couldn't be sure whether we really understood what he was trying to say to us or if he was grasping accurately what we had communicated to him. But at least he could understand just by watching what we were doing here, and we could understand what he was doing. That was enough for the time being.

About four o'clock in the morning, Minister Golborne passed by. Approaching the campfire, he thanked the group for holding the prayer vigil and for the support their actions provided for the miners. Someone offered him a cup of herbal tea. Folding his hands around the cup to warm them, he sipped the fragrant liquid with appreciation. After all these weeks, he was no longer just a high government functionary but a neighbor and friend, his demeanor gracious and kind.

A wealthy Chilean business executive, Minister Golborne had never worked in the mining industry until being appointed to his present position by the newly elected President Piñera less than a year earlier. Much of the Chilean public had grumbled over the appointment of a man with no experience in Chile's chief industry. But after he had handled the crisis with so much determination, courage, and compassion, his popularity had risen as high among the Chilean people beyond San José Mine as among the Camp Hope residents themselves.

After drinking his tea, Minister Golborne continued on his way, stopping often to chat with the miners' relatives he encountered along the way. Meanwhile, María Segovia, worn out from so many hours without sleep, always active and helping those with needs, fell asleep next to the fire. Since her brother Dario wasn't scheduled to be raised to the surface until the next day, some of the prayer vigil group suggested she retire to her own tent for an undisturbed rest. But she refused, determined to remain on duty and vigilant, just as she had been all these weeks, until the last miner emerged to safety. So we let her rest by the fire, doing our best not to disturb her.

The prayer vigil bonfire that last night became a focal point for the camp residents, a gathering place where we could find warmth for our chilled bodies in the cold desert night, but an even greater spiritual and emotional warmth to revitalize our faith during those final hours. Men, women, children, the elderly, family members, rescue personnel, volunteers, and visitors all drifted over to take their turn around its flames. As they listened to the singing and participated in the prayers, they went on their way with hearts uplifted and with renewed hope.

Despite the good progress, everyone couldn't help feeling a certain anxiety. Something could easily go wrong with the shaft, the Phoenix capsule, the cable that had to raise and lower the capsule, or the miners themselves. So many risks. But at that moment there was none of the anguish that had assaulted us all, especially the family members, over the last sixty-nine days. God had watched over the miners to this moment. How could we not trust Him to watch over them until the end when so little now remained to finish the task?

15

THE RESCUE

The final rescue began just before midnight, the morning of October 13. All the many daily miracles we'd witnessed to date had been building up to this greatest one: the rescue of all thirty-three miners. If everything went well, they would now emerge one by one from the dark prison where they'd been held captive for more than two months.

The process of the extraction was well organized. A bright glare of floodlights turned the top of the mountain bright as day. All the various teams of rescue personnel, identified by their neon-orange outfits and white helmets, stood on alert. A medical official stood out among them in an all-white jumpsuit and helmet. Close to the platform where the Phoenix capsule would be winched into the mouth of the shaft, a roofed shelter had been built for observers. These included President Piñera and other dignitaries, along with two family members chosen by each miner, who would take their turn in the shelter when their loved one was scheduled to emerge.

The rest of the family members remained down in the camp watching on their own televisions or on the huge movie screen erected in front of the dining tent so that everyone could view the exit of each miner. As the countdown began, family members and friends spontaneously divided themselves into separate groups. As camp chaplain, I had come to know these families well over the last ten weeks. Moving from one family to another, I visited with them and prayed, offering help and comfort in any way I could.

The rescue personnel who would oversee the extraction had already descended safely into the mine. The Phoenix capsule seemed to be working smoothly. The shaft was not straight down but on a steep diagonal with slight bends and turns that had been necessary to correct the course during the drilling process. Retractable wheels permitted the rocket-shaped device to scoot easily over the turns and protected it from bumping into the sides of the shaft.

The first miner scheduled to emerge was Florencio Ávalos, a shift supervisor second in rank to the foreman, Luis Urzúa. I stood together with the Ávalos family as we watched the Phoenix capsule, painted red, white, and blue for the colors of the Chilean flag, descend into the shaft. A video camera allowed us to see the capsule reaching the bottom of the mine. The cheers began as Florencio stepped into the capsule and its mesh door closed behind him. Then came the complete concentration of suspense as the Phoenix capsule was drawn up the shaft. An accident inside the shaft or a malfunction of the system was still always possible. Who could predict what might happen?

The time was 12:15 a.m. on October 13, when the powerful winch slowly lifted the capsule clear of the narrow hole in the ground, looking no bigger on the TV screen than a chimney flue. As the rescue workers grabbed it and settled it to the platform, the mesh door opened. A great celebration erupted as Florencio stepped free. The first miner was safe!

Florencio was wearing the green jumpsuit, a miner's helmet, and Oakley sunglasses provided by the rescue team. But over the jumpsuit, he was also wearing another article of clothing: a tan T-shirt. On the front of the T-shirt was a white star against a red and blue background, representing the Chilean flag. Above the star were the words *"¡Gracias, Señor!"* or "Thank You, Lord!"

As he stooped to hug his nine-year-old son and his wife, words printed on the back became visible: "In His hand are the depths of the earth, and the mountain peaks belong to Him."

The quotation was from Psalm 95:4. The T-shirts had been gifts to the miners from the Chilean branch of a Christian student organization, Campus Crusade, along with MP3 players that held an audio version of the *Jesus* film and a Spanish audio version of the New Testament. Along with the miniature Bibles I'd been able to send down, the miners had expressed repeatedly how being able to listen to the story of Jesus Christ had been a spiritual comfort to them during their captivity. Most of the miners chose to wear those T-shirts over their green overalls during their ride to the surface as a declaration of their thanksgiving and gratitude to God for the miracle of their rescue.

Once Florencio had hugged his family, he was quickly strapped to a stretcher and transported by a team of paramedics to the field clinic. All across the camp, the television crews were transmitting

live the details of the first successful rescue, the voices of the journalists choked with emotion as though they were reporting on one of
their own family members. Indeed, these trapped men had become
family to those so closely involved in their rescue all these weeks.
Meanwhile, around the world, it was estimated that an audience of
more than a billion people were watching the live coverage of the
rescue, cheering and praying.

Mario Sepúlveda was the second to emerge. A big, energetic
man, he was famous for being a jokester, and as the Phoenix capsule neared the surface, he could be heard over the video connection
chanting joyously: "Get me out of here! Get me out of here!"

It lessened the tension, making everyone laugh. He continued to make humorous remarks that had everyone chuckling as
the capsule emerged from the shaft. As soon as the mesh door
opened, Mario sprang out without waiting for help from the rescue personnel and began hugging everyone in sight: his wife, his
son, President Piñera, Minister Golborne, rescue operations chief
André Sougarret, and even the president's wife.

Opening a bag, he held up small pyrite-studded rocks from
the bottom of the mine, which he distributed as souvenirs, beginning with President Piñera. Then he ran enthusiastically toward
the barrier that separated the rescue operation from the rest of the
crowd. Shaking hands and hugging those close enough to reach,
he led the crowd in a cheer. "Chi-chi-chi! Le-le-le! Chile!"

Mario Sepúlveda was one of the miners for whom this terrible
experience had brought a life-changing spiritual impact. "I was
with God and the devil, and they fought over me," he'd shared,
"and God won!"

Juan Illanes and Carlos Mamani, the single Bolivian in the

group, were raised to the surface without incident. I followed with close attention the ascent of Jimmy Sánchez, the fifth scheduled to be raised. At nineteen years old, he was the youngest of the miners. His home was in Villa Esperanza, a neighborhood of Copiapó. He had been the first to communicate to those on the surface his conviction that God was the thirty-fourth Miner among them. The difference was that God wasn't trapped by the mine collapse as they were but had voluntarily chosen to be present with them at every moment to help them and keep them safe.

Jimmy had given testimony to this conviction in a letter he sent me from below, written out on plain graph paper torn from a mathematics notebook. The following is what he wrote me:

"Dear Pastor Parra, I thank you from my heart for all the help you have been giving to my family and of course to all of us. All that remains now is to keep praying much for the help of our Lord that all will end well. We are all well here, thanks to God who has not for a single moment abandoned us. So we truly are '34' because God never left our side. Thank you again for everything, Jimmy Sánchez."

Along the left border of his note, Jimmy had added, "PS. All of this is God's work, and to Him I give thanks for everything."

As the camp chaplain, I stayed with each family as their miner was being raised from captivity. The next to be announced was Osmar Araya, followed by José Ricardo Ojeda. José was the miner who had taped the message to the drill head that let everyone know all thirty-three were alive and safe in the emergency shelter. As a diabetic, his survival had been made possible by the medicines sent down through the *paloma*. He had celebrated his forty-seventh birthday on Monday, October 11, while still waiting for rescue, his companions jokingly promising him a sugar-free cake once he was out of the mine.

José was also one of the men who had written me a personal letter from down in the mine. A widower, he had no biological children, but a stepdaughter he'd raised as his own. She was waiting for him along with two nephews and other family members. As I joined the family, I was still carrying his letter with me.

When I'd read his letter, I was deeply touched by the profound spirituality of this hardworking, blue-collar laborer, his deep faith and close relationship with God shining through every word of his simple phrases. Standing with other family members, I commented, "I received a wonderful letter from José Ojeda while he was in the mine. In fact, I have it with me."

The Chile National TV Network was broadcasting live a description of José's rescue very close to where we were standing. Hearing my comment, one of the news crew spun around and interrupted the reporter, "Hey, look, the pastor has a letter from José Ojeda."

The transmission was momentarily on pause since the central station in Santiago was in the middle of a commercial break. The reporter approached me. "Pastor, would you mind if we did a news interview with this letter?"

The letter was nothing José Ojeda had intended to keep private, so I responded, "Certainly, if you wish."

When the broadcast resumed, the news crew focused a camera in on the letter while the commentator announced, "We are here with Pastor Carlos Parra who has been the chaplain of Camp Hope. He has here a letter which José Ricardo Ojeda, who is now ascending from the mine, wrote to him. Pastor—"

Here the news commentator turned to me. "Would you mind reading to us the contents of that letter?"

With my own emotions barely contained, I read the letter aloud:

Pastor Carlos Parra Díaz:

From here below I thank you and your family for your constant prayers on behalf of us the 33 miners. I can share that here we are all calm and confident that God Almighty has protected us from the very first day that all this has happened. I can report that down here we too pray at 12:00 noon every day of our captivity.

Down here below there is every kind of creed and denomination among us. But we are all brothers in God. I am finding it a little difficult to write ... something within me is making it hard to think clearly. But if God has preserved us with life, it is because He is preparing us for something when we get out. Down here there is much time to think and pray.

To you and your family, I can testify that only Jesus Christ gives us rest and peace so that our heavy burden down here becomes something light to bear. Because of this, we see opening ahead of us a future filled with hope where our current afflictions have been transformed into comfort.

I bid farewell to you and all of your family.

José Ricardo Ojeda V.,

'Corazón de Minero'

Corazón de Minero or "Heart of a Miner" was a nickname that had been given to José Ojeda by his peers because of his courage and patient endurance. I know that the sincere faith of his words impacted many who heard them on the broadcast. But it was my own heart that was once again deeply touched as I read them aloud. José waved a Chilean flag as he stepped out of the capsule and then hugged his stepdaughter, whom he had chosen to be present on the platform to greet him.

16

SUCCESS!

After José Ojeda followed Claudio Yañez and Mario Gómez. Then came the turn of Alex Vega, age thirty-two. His father José Vega, a retired miner, had rushed to San José Mine when news came of the disaster. Strong and capable at seventy years old, he had taken his own crew of five into the mouth of the mine, looking for a way down to his son, but further avalanches had driven him back. I spent time with Alex Vega's family, chatting with one of his uncles, Señor Plaza.

"When is Alex scheduled to ascend?" I asked him.

"About 9:30 in the morning it will be his turn," he answered.

"That's just a short time away," I commented.

He gave me a big hug. His eyes filled with tears, and he said fervently, "Pastor Parra, I just want to express my appreciation for the spiritual support that you have offered to our family these past sixty-nine days. Thank you for sending the Bible to my nephew. Thank you so much! Thank you, thank you."

He kept repeating his thanks. Just then they announced the ascent of Alex. His family members were all gathered in front of the giant TV screen except for his wife, who was waiting to greet him on the platform. Like so many others, Alex had chosen to wear over his green jumpsuit the tan T-shirt that gave thanks to God. By now the sun had risen again, hot and bright overhead, and his polarized sunglasses had turned very dark to protect his eyes. He hugged his wife Jessica for a long moment as the crowd cheered. Then as he finally stepped away, he stretched out the front of his T-shirt in a display of the words, "*Gracias, Señor.* Thank You, Lord."

The rescue personnel were now securing him onto a stretcher to take him to the field hospital. At that moment Alex raised a hand high. In his hand was the miniature Bible we had been able to send down to the miners. As the stretcher moved down from the rescue platform, Alex grabbed the Bible as well with his second hand, waving the tiny black book like a victory trophy.

His action, as though offering unspoken testimony to the miracle of his rescue, touched my emotions profoundly. This time it was my turn to let the tears come to my eyes. I cried like a baby. I called Gloria, my wife, on my cell phone. She had been awake through the night. All of Chile was accompanying the miners as each one rose to the surface.

"Lolita," I said, using my pet name for her, "did you see Alex Vega emerge with his Bible in his hand?"

"Yes, I saw," she responded. We talked briefly about the miners and the extraordinary miracle of their rescue.

I returned then to Señor Plaza, who was also weeping freely. Giving him a big hug, I asked him, "Did you see Alex with the Bible in his hand?"

"Yes, Pastor, I saw it. It was as though he was communicating that the victory today came from God."

After Alex Vega, others emerged one by one. Jorge Galleguillos, who had witnessed the white butterfly. Edison Peña, whose wife Angélica had inscribed a testimony to her faith in his rescue on a boulder. Carlos Barrios. Victor Zamora. Victor Segovia. Daniel Herrera.

Omar Reygadas, who had helped José Henríquez give spiritual leadership to the trapped miners, was number seventeen. A 56-year-old widower with six children, fourteen grandchildren, and four great-grandchildren, he had been a miner for three decades and had been trapped underground twice before, though only briefly. Omar too gave immediate testimony to the faith that had sustained him during his long days of captivity, kneeling in front of everyone to pray, the miniature Bible he'd received raised high in his right hand.

After Esteban Rojas and Pablo Rojas, who were cousins, came the twentieth miner to be rescued, Dario Segovia, brother of María Segovia, at 4 p.m. The Segovias were a large family. Forty-eight years old, Dario was one of thirteen siblings and had six children himself. He'd been a prolific letter writer during his time in the mine, including to his sister María, Camp Hope's beloved "mayor." In his letters he'd expressed how he had found God through this difficult experience.

As he reached the surface, Dario tried to remove the Oakley sunglasses, which he'd been ordered to keep on to avoid damaging his eyes as they were exposed to sunlight after so many days underground. The crowd could see his action as the capsule was maneuvered clear of the shaft. Immediately they began shouting, "Don't take off the glasses!"

The rescue crew opened the door. Dario had a Chilean flag draped around his neck over the now usual tan T-shirt proclaiming thanksgiving to God. Even before greeting his wife, he placed the flag on the ground, knelt down, and, throwing his hands high toward heaven, called out, "Thank you, God!"

Then he rose to hug his wife and continued on with the protocol of stretcher and medical care. Down below, watching his release on the giant TV screen, were the many members of Dario's large family, including María Segovia. Because of María's presence, the media crews were crowding around them even more than had been the case with the other families. Everyone wanted a statement from María as her brother emerged from the mine. I was standing at her side at the time. As María gave a statement to the journalists, she gestured toward me.

"Faith has been very important. We have been holding a prayer vigil here with Pastor Parra, who has been with us since the beginning. We give thanks to God because all of this is a miracle, that my brother has emerged alive."

I had not seen this forceful, decisive woman who had shown such leadership at Camp Hope ever cry in all the long weeks of waiting. But now suddenly she was weeping. In happiness, certainly, in relief for an end to the long stress, in gratitude to God. And perhaps because she had not yet had opportunity to hug her brother and express her emotion to him. Was Dario aware of all that María had done to sustain the hopes of everyone in the camp? Of all that she had done for him specifically in those critical moments of pushing the mine owners and rescue crews to press forward in looking for the trapped men and not give up? Once again I found tears streaming down my face as we all sought to comfort her.

Soon after Dario reached the surface, María left Camp Hope to head back to her home in Antofagasta. She did so without any fanfare, so modestly and quietly we didn't even know when she left. In the height of her leadership at Camp Hope, many of the residents had insisted that she needed to continue her new career after the rescue was over.

"When we have the next elections," they would tell her, "you should present yourself as a candidate for mayor of your municipality, perhaps even for city council."

María always responded the same way. "None of that. I am not a politician. I will return to Antofagasta where I live and return to my food stand in the marketplace. I will keep selling my *empanadas* as I always have. That is something I do very well, and I am happy to do so."

María Segovia wasn't the only person who spent long weeks at Camp Hope for no personal attention or glory but only to serve others. There were many, each one carrying out their own part of this difficult mission, thinking only of the thirty-three men and the urgency of their rescue. That unity of purpose and action was in itself a miracle—the miracle of selflessness, of sacrificial love.

More miners followed Dario to freedom. Yonni Barrios. Samuel Ávalos. Carlos Bugueño. José Henríquez, the godly Christian man who had been the miners' pastor underground. Renan Ávalos, brother of Florencio, the first miner who had emerged.

Claudio Acuña. Franklin Lobos, the former professional soccer player who had been driving the pickup truck when he and Jorge Galleguillos saw the white butterfly.

Another poignant moment occurred when the twenty-eighth miner emerged. Awaiting 23-year-old Richard Villarroel were his mother, a brother, and his younger sister. Eleven years old with long black hair and dark eyes, Richard's little sister held up a Chilean flag with the names of each of the miners written on it, a beaming smile on her face even while tears spilled from her eyes. Because of the danger of his job, Richard had never told his mother where he worked, though he'd now been a miner for two years. His mother and other family members had found out only when they were contacted and told that Richard was among the men trapped in San José Mine.

Waving her flag as she waited for her brother to emerge, the little girl initiated the traditional cheer: "Chi-chi-chi! Le-le-le!"

Enchanted with the little girl, the crowd joined in. Standing to one side was the rescue coordinator, André Sougarret, waiting to greet Richard as he had each of the miners when they emerged. A serious man who rarely smiled or showed emotion during the long weeks of the rescue operation, André Sougarret is a perfectionist in his work, the consummate mining professional as might be expected of a top executive of Codelco, the Chilean state mining company. When President Piñera placed him in charge of the rescue, he took on the enormous challenge unflinchingly, becoming the brains behind the most complex rescue in the history of mining.

While the trapped miners rose to the surface one by one, the rescue coordinator had remained vigilant and composed on the rescue platform. But as Richard Villarroel hugged his mother and little sister, André Sougarret let his emotions spill over, tears standing in his eyes as he watched the reunion of this family. All his hard work, all the long days and nights, the difficult challenges, his own worries as to whether he could actually pull off the operation, had led to this. New life, not just for these trapped men, but for their families who had missed them so much as well.

After Richard Villarroel came Juan Aguilar, Raúl Bustos, Pedro Cortez, and Ariel Ticona. Ariel's wife, Elizabeth, was there to greet him, though baby Esperanza had not made the trip.

Then came the final miner.

Night had once again fallen over the desert. As one billion people watched around the world, the Phoenix capsule rumbled down into the mine and then began its slow ascent. In it was Luis Urzúa, fifty-four years old, foreman of the shift that had entered San José Mine on August 5, expecting to be there twelve hours, a shift which had now extended to sixty-nine days.

As shift foreman, Luis Urzúa had been the de facto commander-in-chief of the thirty-three miners during their ten weeks underground, a responsibility he'd taken very seriously. Now as his final act of leadership, he'd insisted on being the last miner to ascend to the surface. When he reached the surface at 9:55 p.m., October 13, all of Chile filled with cheers, horns honking, bells ringing, making every kind of noise in an expression of sheer joy. At Camp Hope, flags waved, confetti rained down on the families, and thirty-three balloons in the red, white, and blue of the Chilean flag were released in celebration of the successful rescue.

After hugging family and rescuers, Luis Urzúa stepped forward to greet the Chilean president, Sebastián Piñera, his words forceful and clear: "Mr. President, I deliver to you my shift. I hope something like this will never happen again. I am grateful and proud for all that you have accomplished here. Thank you to the rescue crews. Thank you to all of Chile and to the many people who have contributed to this rescue. I am delighted to be a Chilean and proud to live in this country. On behalf of all my men who are with me today, safe and sound, thanks to you: Thank you, thank you."

"Don Luis Urzúa," President Piñera responded, "I accept the delivery of your shift and congratulate you for having completed your mission, emerging last of your men as any good captain does. I want to say to you, Don Luis, that we the Chilean people are very proud of you and of all of the thirty-three miners. You have given us all a model for friendship, courage, and loyalty. Here in front of you, I want to express as well my gratitude to all the thousands of personnel who have worked unceasingly so that all of you might be here today with us."

The president went on to enumerate one by one all the individuals and groups who had been working on behalf of the miners. He finished his statement by saying, "And I want also to give thanks to Someone who helped us at every turn. I want to thank God Almighty who was with all of us constantly." Inviting the shift foreman to stand at his side, President Piñera then led the entire crowd in singing the national anthem. The crowd joined in, then finished their singing once more with the triumphant chant, "Chi-chi-chi! Le-le-le!"

Not long after the rescue, Luis Urzúa was invited to speak during a world tour which had been arranged for the rescued miners. He described the astonishing success of the rescue, the emergence of all thirty-three men from the mine, as a resurrection. "The hand of God was in this," Luis Urzúa stated unequivocally. "The thirty-fourth Miner down there with us was God."

This recognition of divine intervention throughout the entire process of the rescue has been the consistent perspective of the miners, their families, the rescue personnel, and millions around the world who became witnesses to God's hand at work as they followed the story of thirty-three men trapped beneath the earth and the miracle of their restoration to life.

17

THANKSGIVING
AND PRAISE TO GOD

Once the last trapped miner had been freed, the rescue personnel too were brought to the surface. With the last man out of the mine, the dismantling of Camp Hope began at once. The miners themselves were airlifted to a hospital in Copiapó. Thanks to the care of the medical personnel who had been attending them from the surface, the miners had emerged in surprisingly good health. Still, the high humidity and heat, so many long days in captivity, and the initial seventeen days of malnourishment had left their mark. The medical authorities were determined to ensure that all was well with the men before releasing them to their families.

Because throngs of well-wishers as well as media crews had mobbed the hospital, a protective cordon was established to keep the miners from being overwhelmed by publicity. Access to the hospital wing where they were being housed was available only to a few professionals—medical personnel, psychologists, pastors— along with immediate family. As chaplain of Camp Hope, I was among the pastors invited to offer spiritual counsel to the miners in the aftermath of their ordeal. Visiting the miners, I encountered again the rescue operation's chief medical officer, Dr. Jean Romagnoli, and their psychologist, Dr. Alberto Iturra. Both had returned to their own practices but continued to attend the miners as well.

The miners were housed in two separate wards on the third floor of the hospital. I already knew each miner by sight and had communicated in writing and by videoconference with a number of them. But we had not met personally. As I visited each miner at the hospital, the quickest way to establish a connection was in reference to the miniature Bible that had been sent down to them. The moment I introduced myself as Pastor Parra who had sent the Bibles, an immediate bond was established, their appreciation and pleasure manifest as we spoke. During the first day, I visited with sixteen miners. The next day I visited with the others. All appeared healthy and voiced deep gratitude to God for their rescue. They shared how they had studied the Bible and prayed regularly and told me how their faith in God had helped keep up their hopes and maintained a spirit of trust among them while they were underground.

Among the men I visited was Ariel Ticona, the father of baby Esperanza and nephew of Héctor Ticona, a member of one of my congregations. As we shared together how I had visited his wife and newborn daughter in the hospital, Ariel began pouring out all that was on his heart: the joy he'd felt in witnessing his daughter's birth from underground, the thoughts of hope and comfort that had kept him from giving up, his determination to keep fighting to stay alive so that he could hold his daughter and protect her as a father, and his anxiety and frustration at not being with his wife to take care of her as her time came.

Now all this was once again possible because he was outside and free. Soon he would be able to return to being a husband and father, caring for his loved ones without any further limitation. Months later, I was able to follow up on Ariel and Elizabeth and their daughter, Esperanza. They continue to rejoice in their new life together as a family and to give thanks to God for bringing them back together.

It was a special pleasure to visit as well with José Henríquez, the "pastor" of the trapped miners. He was among those I'd been able to speak with while they were still underground. He'd shared with me about their difficult survival during those first seventeen days when they had no contact with the outside. From the beginning José had proposed to the group to set aside a certain time each day for prayer, and all had accepted. When they came together to pray, he would recite certain Bible texts that he knew from memory. But his repertoire of memorized verses was soon exhausted. The group had longed for a Bible so they might read more of God's Word. Like all their other needs at that time, it had seemed a wish that could never be fulfilled. Then four days after they'd been found alive, the miniature Bibles arrived below, a direct answer to their prayers. Their communal prayer times at midday and 6 p.m. were greatly enriched, José told me, because they were all able to read God's Word for themselves at any moment of the day they felt a need. And those moments, he added, were many.

The miners spent two days in the hospital to complete the various medical exams. On the fourth day after the rescue, once the miners had been released, a commemorative thanksgiving service took place on the site of what had been Camp Hope. The choice of location came from the miners. They had not yet seen the place that held such significance to their family members. When they'd emerged from the mine, they had been moved by stretcher directly to the field clinic and then flown by helicopter to the hospital in Copiapó. Now they wanted to see for themselves the site where their families had kept vigil for so many weeks.

As the Camp Hope chaplain, it fell to me to coordinate the event. Many organizations, both religious and political, from the regional governor, senators, and congressmen to the president of the Association of Evangelical Pastors of Copiapó and the Catholic bishop of Copiapó, as well as many of the rescued miners and their families, participated in the celebration. It was decided that the thanksgiving ceremony should also be an official act of closure for Camp Hope. Our purpose was to give thanks to God for the successful conclusion of the rescue operation and to bring together the miners with their families, even if only this one time, on the site where both families and miners had not only suffered so much but had celebrated such a joyous resurrection to a new life.

The thanksgiving service took place Sunday, October 17, at 10:00 in the morning. Already very little remained of what had been a busy town with thousands of residents. A tent was raised on the empty clearing where Camp Hope had been. Police kept reporters from intruding on the service. The program included participation by various churches and denominations represented among the miners. First the Catholic bishop, Monsignor Duarte, offered a mass. Then the Asaf Quartet, which had held a concert weeks earlier at Camp Hope, sang the Lord's Prayer. This was followed by a speech from the local governor, Mrs. Ximena Matas, centered on thanksgiving to God for the miracle He had brought about.

A representative from the families spoke next. The representative chosen was Alex Vega's uncle, Señor Plaza, who had shed tears of joy and relief when his nephew waved his Bible from his stretcher while being carried to the field clinic. Señor Plaza gave thanks to God for having protected his nephew and all thirty-three miners.

For a devotional meditation that followed, I had chosen Psalm 40:1–3, the passage that had become so significant to the miners buried deep in their own wet and slimy pit of despair: "I waited patiently for the Lord; he turned to me and heard my cry. He lifted me out of the slimy pit, out of the mud and mire."

As representative of the miners themselves, we had hoped to invite their spiritual leader, José Henríquez. José was not able to be present, but Carlos Mamani, the single Bolivian among the trapped miners, had volunteered to take his place. In his speech, he shared, "God has rescued us, and I want to surrender my heart to Him. I also want to testify to all the world that it was God who delivered us from the pit."

When he had finished, I asked if any other miner wished to speak. Two raised their hands. Luis Urzúa, the shift foreman, spoke first. He shared how God had done so many things for the trapped miners, giving them strength and sustaining them, and thanked God for the miracle He had undertaken in bringing out alive all thirty-three miners. After he finished, Omar Reygadas spoke. It was Omar who had immediately knelt with his Bible uplifted toward heaven when he'd emerged from the Phoenix capsule. He shared how God had given him the strength and hope to resist until the end and that for the rest of his life he wanted to raise high the name of the Lord.

Rev. Sergio Soriano, president of the Association of Evangelical Pastors of Copiapó, offered the closing prayer, thanking God once again for this miracle. The commemorative service ended with a special number sung by Javier Beroiza from Santiago, entitled "Faith Can Move Mountains."

This was a phrase the family members of the miners had repeated countless times during their long wait. While he sang, they clapped out the beat enthusiastically. As the service ended, Javier sang the song one more time while more than 600 people who had gathered for the service hugged each other in joy for what God had done in this place.

The focus for the miners and their families shifted next to Santiago, where a number of commemorative celebrations were held to honor them. Eduardo Durán, the senior pastor of the Evangelical Cathedral of Santiago, had invited all the miners for a special thanksgiving service on Sunday, October 24. The largest evangelical church in Santiago, the cathedral occupies an entire city block on the historic Avenue Libertador Bernardo O'Higgins with a seating of 16,000 and an attendance in its multiple services of 45,000.

Invited to take part were the thirty-three miners, Minister of Mines Laurence Golborne, the various mayors of the zone of San

José Mine, the rescue teams, various other authorities, and myself as chaplain of Camp Hope. About 7000 people were in attendance. I opened the service with a brief message which included a video containing clips of significant moments from the long days of the miners' captivity. When I finished my part, the thirty-three miners entered with Mrs. Ximena Matas, and the provincial governor of the entire Atacama region, Nicolás Noman. The audience welcomed them with prolonged applause. Senior Pastor Eduardo Durán presented a large Bible to each of the miners. Several of the miners spoke briefly. At the very end, I too was presented with a large Bible with my name engraved on it in gold letters.

On Monday, October 25, President Sebastian Piñera hosted a special presentation for the miners in the Palace of La Moneda, seat of Chile's national government. The president gave a short speech emphasizing the wholehearted efforts of the entire country in the rescue and renewing the commitment of his administration to improve safety measures for all of Chile's miners. Then he bestowed on each of the thirty-three miners a presidential medal and a miniature copy of the Phoenix capsule.

They all dined together in the palace and then in the afternoon played a game of soccer in the National Stadium. One team was assembled from among the miners, the other from the rescue team, including President Piñera, Minister Golborne, and rescue coordinator André Sougarret. Despite the coaching of former soccer star Franklin Lobos on the miners' side, the rescue team won, 3–2. The miners didn't mind. Their own victory had been their release from captivity, a victory also for the rescue team. Both teams celebrated amicably together afterwards.

On Tuesday, October 26, the thirty-three miners traveled

to Valparaíso, seat of Chile's national congress, about 120 kilometers from Santiago, for an award ceremony where they were each honored with a bicentennial medal, given as a recognition of the endurance and courage they had displayed during their long captivity. So ended the official celebrations. But the story of the thirty-three miners will never be finished, as neither their lives nor the lives of those who came in contact with them over those ten weeks will ever be the same.

18

FINAL REFLECTIONS

L ike the rescue crews, medical personnel, and family members, I too headed home once the rescue operation was over. My life quickly returned to its daily routine: tending to the needs of my congregations around Copiapó and spending time again with my wife and children. But I myself had changed as well, my life and heart permanently altered by the experience of those ten weeks. I had always believed that God is real, a living God who chooses to be close to those who love Him. But during my weeks at Camp Hope, I experienced for myself, far more than I'd ever dreamed possible, just how real God is, how deeply He loves the human beings He has created, how directly involved He is in the daily lives of His children.

I'd once stood on a hilltop outside Copiapó, praying that God would give me opportunity to lift high to all nations the name of Jesus Christ, who laid down His life for my sins on a cross far less picturesque than the painted white symbol atop Cerro de la Cruz, the Hilltop of the Cross. Now what burned in me was the urgency of the message God had placed on my heart.

That urgency has continued to grow in my heart through the months since the successful conclusion of the San José Mine rescue. I think of the earthquake, 8.8 on the Richter scale, that devastated Chile just six months before the San José Mine disaster; the earthquake that destroyed much of Haiti only six weeks before that; the Indian Ocean tsunami one day after Christmas in 2004 that left millions homeless across Indonesia, Sri Lanka, and other Asian nations. Now even as I finish telling my story, a 9.0 magnitude earthquake has devastated Japan, again leaving countless thousands dead, missing, or displaced. The news brings sharply to my mind the words of Jesus Christ Himself in the Gospel of Matthew when His disciples asked Him for the signs that would mark His return and the ending of this present age. Among those signs, Jesus had told them, would be great famines and earthquakes (Matthew 24:7).

In the midst of all these terrible tragedies, I ask myself, why does the story of San José Mine stand out in such contrast? Why did God permit this disaster to happen in the first place? Why focus the eyes of the world, of more than a billion people who watched the events unfold, on this single happening? Why such an incredible and miraculous happy ending to this particular story? If, as so many believe, we are indeed in the last days of this present world, what is the message God is seeking to communicate through this experience?

Sometime after the dismantling of Camp Hope, I drove out

one last time to San José Mine. The narrow highway was just as it had been: dusty, bumpy, twisting around tight curves. The distant peaks of the Andes rose high and snowcapped against a cloudless sky. In my many other trips out there, I'd rarely seen them. Not because they'd been hidden by clouds; the days had always been clear and bright. But with my thoughts focused on the tragedy of the miners, I had paid little attention to my surroundings. Today they were starkly beautiful against the sky. The desert landscape stretching empty and silent away from me radiated a tranquil peace.

As I rounded the final bends of the road, I began to feel the uncharacteristic silence, the lonely solitude of the mine. Memories of Camp Hope as I had known it came flooding back. The sky-blue dining tent, looming impressively large over the rest of the camp, should have been just beyond this curve. But it wasn't there. I turned my head to take in where campfires had flickered cheerfully in front of each small family shelter. But they weren't there either.

Just ahead there should have been a labyrinth of communication equipment: portable towers, antennas, satellite dishes, huge television screens, the tangle of snakelike cables. But there was nothing. The platform area in front of the dining tent where we had held prayer vigils, celebrations, and concerts was now just a bare piece of earth. I looked up at the hilltop where a semicircle of Chilean flags had waved in the breeze, in token of the prayers being raised to heaven on behalf of the miners. All I saw was a gray, rocky knoll, just like every other one in sight.

The San José Mine itself was now closed to further mining. At the very end of the road, a barrier still remained, blocking off the mouth of the mine. The shafts drilled down into the earth had been covered over to keep anyone from falling in. The drilling rigs, backhoes, vehicles, and all the other equipment were gone as well. Only a unit of police officers remained on duty to prevent the curious from exploring the dangerous interior of the mine.

What happened with everything that was here? I found myself asking. *So much that was here, all those people, how could it all just disappear as though it had never been?*

I knew the answer, of course. Camp Hope had served its purpose. Its residents were now back where they belonged in their own homes, whether in towns nearby or far distant from this place. The hundreds of news crews who'd covered the rescue operation had now moved on to the next big story.

And yet, in a very real way, Camp Hope still existed in the hearts and lives of all who had been among its inhabitants. The hope that was its spirit. The faith, so strong and unyielding, that had been demonstrated among family members and rescue personnel alike. The unity of purpose that had brought together those who were here as one family. That constant conversation with God by means of prayer we all experienced, both on the surface and among the miners deep underground, for the entirety of those sixty-nine days. None of this would be forgotten so long as the story of this place continued to be told.

The miners themselves have also moved on with their lives. Some have taken new jobs. Others have retired completely from mining. Many have traveled extensively since their rescue, sharing their experience with audiences around the world. In the months since Camp Hope closed down, I have had opportunity to visit with some of the miners and to hear from others. I spent time with Jimmy Sánchez, the youngest miner, who first expressed his conviction that God was the "thirty-fourth Miner" present with them down in the mine. He shared with me that he feels he has truly been given a new life and that he is determined to live his new life for God.

I visited with Mario Sepúlveda and his family in Santiago. Mario had once shared that God and the devil had fought over him, and God won. Now he told me of his determination to spend the rest of his life telling the world that God does indeed exist and cares for mankind.

While I have not had opportunity to visit again with María Segovia, Camp Hope's beloved "mayor," since she returned to Antofagasta, 500 kilometers from Copiapó, I have received word of how she continues to share her gratitude to God for His miracle in bringing home safely her brother Dario and all the rest of "the boys," as she always refers to the miners. I have spent time also in the Ticona family home. Ariel and Elizabeth with their baby daughter, Esperanza, continue to do well. Ariel's father, Héctor, and the entire family continue to rejoice in answered prayer and to be much involved in their local church.

I have visited as well with Víctor Zamora. The fourteenth man to be rescued, Víctor was not actually a miner at all but a mechanic, underground that day to repair a vehicle. He had come to work at San José Mine only because his home had been among those destroyed by the earthquake six months earlier. His wife, Jessica, had just found out that she was three months pregnant with their second child at the time of the mine collapse. Their young son was there with her to greet Víctor when he emerged from underground.

A very active, always busy man, Víctor Zamora had never considered himself particularly religious. But he too had discovered a profound faith in God through this experience. During his enforced inactivity during the weeks underground, he'd also discovered a gift for poetry, writing dozens of poems about his experience to friends and family aboveground. In one of those poems, he wrote: "Under the earth there is a ray of light, my path, and faith is the last thing that is lost ... I have been born again."

When I spoke with him, Víctor reiterated his newfound faith in God. As he described it, he had been not rescued but reborn. He and his family were committed to a new life of following God. Not long ago, among many international trips the miners have been able to make since their rescue, Víctor and others of the trapped miners were given opportunity to travel around Israel. Víctor Zamora shared, "My favorite place is the road in which our Savior walked, because we [the trapped miners] owe our salvation to Him. It's like getting to know everything He went through to save all people."

For myself, God has also continued to open doors to lift up the name of my Savior among the nations, not just through radio interviews such as I had given while at Camp Hope, but traveling to other countries—the United States, Brazil, El Salvador, Germany, Argentina, and others—to share my own experience at San José Mine and the message God has laid on my heart. In December 2010, I received a request from my denomination to move to Paraguay, to serve as a regional pastor and missionary there. In February 2011, I moved with my family to the Paraguayan capital of Asunción. Although we had never met, my new congregation already knew me well as the chaplain of Camp Hope they'd seen so frequently in the news. As I have shared with them the realness of God, and His closeness to His children, that I had experienced at Camp Hope and the miracle we were privileged to watch God unfold before our eyes, a revival and new commitment to prayer have already become apparent among our congregation.

As in every new place to which I have moved, one of my first actions upon arriving in Asunción was to search out a new hilltop from which to pray. Every Sunday morning at 5:30, I climb to its peak with a group of church members. There we pray for Asunción, for all of Paraguay, for the country's president and government officials, for every citizen that they might come to know God, and for a world beyond Paraguay's borders that is also in need of God's Word and God's love. As I pray, I am reminded of what Angélica Álvarez, wife of miner Edison Peña, once said to me while her husband was still underground: "God has a purpose in all that is happening. God has a great plan in all of this."

As I ponder that purpose—as I ask why God permitted all that happened at San José Mine, the mine collapse, the miners' long captivity, the final successful rescue operation—and as I consider the message God has laid on my own heart, the answer that comes to me is both simple and profound. Here in these last days, in the midst of natural disasters and political turmoil, when we do not know how short a time we have left to answer God's call, God's purpose at San José Mine has been to show the world clearly that He does indeed exist and that He hears the prayers of His people whom He created. Above all, the San José Mine rescue has been an unambiguous message of God's love, not just to the miners and their families, but to a billion people who watched and waited, to an entire world who needed to hear God's voice, to see His caring hand on human lives.

This then is the message of San José Mine: Our God is a God of love. When the trapped miners and their families called out to Him, God did not simply look at faulty human beings, at past failures and mistakes, and abandon them to their fate as unworthy of His intervention. Just as no human father can ignore the tears of his children, so our heavenly Father heard their anguished prayers, and He answered them—as God will hear your prayers and mine, if we will only cry out to Him. Like the loving father in the parable of the prodigal son, like Jesus on the cross on Calvary, God is holding His arms wide to His lost children who have wandered away and forgotten Him, calling for them to return to His loving embrace.

So why did God permit this all to happen?

To get our attention. To call humanity back to Himself. Through the miracle of San José Mine, witnessed by more people than any other news story in history, God has issued a call to His creation, every human being, to make a decision while there is still time to do so. Jesus Christ, the Son of God, laid down His life on the cross as a substitute for sinful humanity, as a guarantee of salvation and eternal life, free of charge, to anyone who will receive this precious gift. By reminding the world of His reality and His love, even in the dark depths of San José Mine, God is offering every human being once again the opportunity to make a very simple decision: Will you follow God, or will You reject Him?

Just as so many of the miners cried out to God in the midst of their suffering, so each of us must make that decision to give our heart and life one hundred percent to God. And we must do so before it is too late. God heard the prayers of thirty-three trapped miners underground. He remained present with them at every moment, the unseen thirty-fourth Miner. He listened to the pleas of their families and a watching world.

And now God waits with His arms spread wide, desiring only one thing: to give new life to those who will receive it. To offer a rebirth, a resurrection, just as He granted when thirty-three miners stepped from darkness into light, from certain death to a new beginning on the rocky slopes of San José Mine that day of October 13, 2010.

How will you respond?